SYNOVIAL SPACE

A GUIDE TO DYNAMIC LIVING

RAPHAEL ST. JAMES

ISBN: 979-8-218-76985-7 (Print)
ISBN: 979-8-218-76986-4 (E-Book)

Design: Roberta Morris, Leave It to 'Berta

Published by Urban Cryo Publishing Inc.
A subsidiary of R&L St. James Holdings Corp.

Synovial Space™ is a registered trademark of H2P Collective Corp. Used under license.

DISCLAIMER

This book provides information, strategies, and exercises for personal development and life improvement. It is intended as educational content only and not as therapeutic advice or professional treatment.

The author draws upon a multifaceted life journey spanning numerous professional fields, including but not limited to licensed massage therapy, movement coaching, and strength and conditioning coaching, hospitality management, real estate, business operations, flexible workspace leadership, administrative coordination, public service, performing arts, activism, permaculture design, and legal studies.

This work is informed by the author's management experiences across diverse environments ranging from luxury hotels and airport spas to nonprofit organizations, government agencies, luxury residential and commercial building hallmarks in New York City, libraries, wellness practices, real estate development, and legal education. This guide transparently shows the methodology supporting the author's audaciously naive resilience, integrating insights gained from his work in roles as varied as operations manager, personal trainer, coach, manual therapist, performer, consultant, student, spoken-word poet, and legal scholar.

The methodologies presented represent the synthesis of this unique constellation of lived experiences, formal education, and continued professional development, reflecting the author's multidimensional approach to life and personal growth.

Despite this wealth of experience, the content does not constitute medical advice, psychological counseling, legal advice, financial planning, or clinical treatment. The exercises, tools, and strategies shared are not intended to diagnose, treat, cure, or prevent any medical or psychological condition.

To Liz,

My anchor, my compass, and the most profound catalyst of my personal growth. For nineteen years, you have seen me at my most vulnerable and my most ambitious, believing in my potential even when I struggled to see it myself. Long before I found the courage to write this book, you were persistently whispering—and sometimes boldly declaring—that my story deserved to be told. Your own journey as a mom, wife, friend, full-time professional, and life coach—balancing passion and purpose across these interconnected roles—has been a living testament to the very principles explored within these pages. This book exists because of your unwavering support, your insight, and your love—a love that has transformed, challenged, and elevated me in ways I could never have imagined.

Weave your dreams through stars and pull tight to connect the light.

Raphael St. James

CONTENTS

FOREWORD

In our journey through life, we often encounter moments that test our strength, challenge our beliefs, and shape our character. It is in these pivotal moments that we discover our true selves and the incredible resilience that lies within us.

This inspiring book, crafted by my husband, Raphael St James, draws from the rich tapestry of his own childhood experiences and career path, offering a profound exploration of resilience and the power of finding space within perceived restrictions. Through these pages, you'll discover how to create "synovial space" - that crucial area of movement and possibility that exists even within apparent confinement.

As you turn the pages of this guide, you will be invited into a world where adversity becomes an opportunity for growth, and limitations transform into steppingstones toward a dynamic and fulfilling life. Whether you're facing physical limitations, career plateaus, emotional challenges, or simply seeking to maximize your potential across all life dimensions, these pages offer practical pathways forward. Each story is a testament to the human spirit's capacity to overcome challenges, encouraging readers to reflect on their own experiences and embrace the lessons learned along the way.

This book is intended to be an interactive guide. It is not merely a collection of anecdotes; it is a workbook designed to engage you actively in the process of self-discovery. Through the lens of the eight pillars of life, you will embark on a journey that encompasses physical movement, mental clarity, emotional intelligence, spiritual connection, professional growth, relational dynamics, financial fluidity, and purposeful living. These pillars form not just a philosophy but a comprehensive system for creating space and movement in every dimension of your life.

This guide is more than just a book; it is a companion for your journey toward dynamic living. It encourages you to ponder, to write, and to take action, fostering a deeper understanding of yourself and the world around you. My husband's authenticity and vulnerability shine through in every story, inspiring you to embrace your own journey with openness and courage. I have seen firsthand how this guide has unfolded even in my personal life, transforming not just individual challenges but our shared vision for what's possible when we approach limitations with curiosity rather than resignation.

As you delve into these pages, I invite you to keep an open heart and mind. Allow the stories to resonate with your own experiences, and let the exercises guide you toward a life filled with purpose and resilience. Together, let us embark on this transformative journey, celebrating the beauty of our shared humanity and the boundless potential that lies within each of us.

Welcome to a path of dynamic living—your adventure begins now! Together, let's discover how to move beyond restrictions and create spaces of possibility in every dimension of your life.

— *Liz St. James*

ACKNOWLEDGMENTS

To those who have passed through the crucible of my life—some by choice, some by circumstance, and some by the cruel hands of fate—this book is a testament to transformation.

To my brother, whose struggle with darkness ultimately illuminated the depths of human resilience. Your absence has been a profound presence, teaching me that pain can be a catalyst for understanding, not just a burden to bear.

To my stepfather, who carried the invisible wounds of 9/11 through mesothelioma, a silent warrior whose strength echoed louder than the towers' fall. Your battle taught me that survival is not about avoiding scars but about how we carry them.

To Mary Jane Tacchi and Sandra Payne at the New York Public Library, my first mentors who saw potential in a young administrative assistant when the world seemed ready to overlook me. You showed me that belief is a powerful act of creation.

To the youth I met at the New York City Housing Authority Youth Chorus, who took in a spoken-word poet and blew my mind with their tremendous display of art. You each propelled me forward in ways words can't express.

To Jim Bonney, who showed me how to transform pain into artistic expression and personal strength through the Meisner acting technique.

To Jane Han, who dared to place me in her documentary, *Urban Scribe*, giving voice to a story waiting to be told.

To Paris, the doorperson from the now-closed Sound Factory—an iconic New York nightclub that lives on in musical legend—who denied my entry on numerous occasions and taught me to never judge a book by its cover. Your repeated rejections became lessons in persistence, humility, and the art of seeing beyond surface appearances.

To Jonathan Peters and Danny Tenaglia—musical architects of the 1990s club scene—who briefly befriended me during a time of profound personal exploration. You were more than DJs; you were alchemists of sound and spirit. In an era riddled with the plague of addiction, my journey through the club scene became a testament to sobriety and self-expression. Music became my definitive solution, a pure mechanism of emotional liberation that transcended the chaos and physical pain of my osteoarthritis.

To every criminal who ever placed a gun to my head, who sought to rob me of my dignity. You became unexpected teachers. In those moments of absolute vulnerability, I learned the difference between victimhood and survival, between fear and resilience.

To the negative personalities I encountered. Thank you for being profound examples of paths I never wanted to walk as I carved out the terrain of who I chose to become.

To the educators who gave a damn—who challenged me to forge truth or risk intellectual evisceration—you taught me that learning is not a passive act but a revolutionary one.

To every error I've made, now transformed into learning experiences. You are not mistakes but stepping stones. Each misstep has fueled every forward movement, every moment of growth.

To my children, Amaya Rushie and Alyssa St. James. You are the most profound teachers of purpose I could have ever imagined. Amaya, as you stand on the cusp of your medical journey beyond St. John's, and Alyssa, with your unwavering academic excellence, you have been my orbit, consistently propelling me toward something far greater than myself. From the moment you both entered my life, you've transformed my understanding of potential, resilience, and unconditional love. Your individual paths are living proof that growth is not about perfection but about persistent, passionate pursuit.

To my osteoarthritis—an unexpected teacher that has become my greatest motivator—you are not my enemy but the fire that ignites my purpose. In the face of physical restrictions, you have transformed my understanding of human potential, driving me to help others move beyond their own limitations while I am still physically able. Your persistent challenge has become my most profound inspiration, proving that constraint can be the catalyst for the most meaningful forms of service.

To God—the architect of the original food forest in the Garden of Eden, and the ultimate source of my ongoing quest for understanding. Though I struggle with your narrative and remain incapable of fully comprehending the complexities of existence, I hold fast to the fundamental truths that whisper of your presence. My journey has been a continuous attempt to return to that primordial state of connection, of pure potential, of harmony between human purpose and divine design.

To standardized tests, which seemed to ludicrously mock me at every turn. You taught me to look past judgment, proving that my worth extends far beyond numerical scores. I am where I am, not because of you but in spite of you.

To my circle of childhood friends who lovingly kept me grounded, reminding me that the world is vast and my perspective is but one thread in an intricate tapestry. Your unwavering honesty has been the mirror that reflects my truest self, challenging me to see beyond my own limited view.

To my wife's extended family who offered me a remarkable transformation from a world where family could be counted on one hand to a vibrant community of over one hundred souls. Each of you has expanded my understanding of love, support, and belonging.

To my sisters-in-law, whose undying love and support have been pillars of strength. Without you, my journey would be unimaginably different.

To my mother-in-law, who at times showed me a depth of maternal love that transcended blood, treating me with a care that spoke volumes about the true meaning of family.

To my father-in-law, who befriended me and treated me as a son despite his uncanny dislike of the long locks of hair I used to wear. Thank you for creating your family.

To my mother, whose struggles and our challenging beginning became powerful reminders of the person I needed to become—a testament to resilience born from understanding what I must not repeat. My love for you transcends the love of a son.

To my biological father, for being authentically himself—your presence, in all its complexity, gifted me with an unshakable, naive resilience that has become my greatest strength.

This book is not just a collection of words but a living testament to the alchemy of human experience—where pain can be transmuted into purpose, and where survival becomes a radical act of creation.

INTRODUCTION
THE DELUGE OF SPACE

WHO THIS JOURNEY IS FOR

This guide is an invitation to those who connect with these conditions:

- Seeking profound personal transformation
- Feeling trapped by life's invisible boundaries
- Yearning to create meaningful movement despite physical or mental limitations
- Turning restrictions into launching points for exceptional growth
- Looking to break through performance plateaus (especially for entrepreneurs and professionals)

WHAT YOU'LL DISCOVER

By the end of our journey together, you'll have the following:

- A revolutionary framework for understanding personal potential and limitation
- Practical tools to navigate life's most challenging restrictions
- A personalized map for creating movement in seemingly impossible spaces
- A deeper understanding of your unique movement architecture
- Actionable strategies for each of the eight pillars of dynamic living

THE PERSONAL ORIGIN: A METHODOLOGY BORN FROM NECESSITY

The first memories of my biological father are etched in the sensory landscape of my childhood apartment in Brooklyn at 594 Driggs Avenue—a world defined by both warmth and absence. Rafael Torres (RIP) was more than a father; he was a momentary beacon of possibility, his smile catching light through the window, his laughter bouncing off narrow walls.

Then came the void—his absence filling that same apartment, transforming it from a home to a landscape of limitation. He wanted to play piano like Mozart for the masses, and I was not part of his quest. The Bible verse from Mark 8:36 echoes in my memory: "What good is it for someone to gain the whole world, yet forfeit their soul?"

My father's choice was a masterclass in restriction—trading away countless precious moments for an undefined dream. But in that space of absence, something profound began to take shape. This early experience taught me that spaces which initially feel empty often contain the greatest potential for movement. Within that void, I discovered my capacity for resilience. This pattern—finding possibility within apparent limitation—became the foundation of the methodology I share with you in this book.

Reflection Prompt

What early experiences of absence or limitation have shaped your understanding of potential?

How have moments of restriction created unexpected space in your life?

The Birth of a Transformational Framework

At seven years old, joint pain from early-onset osteoarthritis began to reshape my understanding of space, movement, and limitation. Each ache was a teacher, each restriction a potential pathway. The physical and social limitations I experienced weren't just obstacles to overcome—they became the very lens through which I began to see all of life's challenges differently. Over years of engaging with various coaching methodologies, I never fully resonated with existing frameworks.

Through my clinical and therapeutic experience as a healer, combined with the sum of my life experiences—my operations management background, entrepreneurial journey, permaculture design, and personal victories and defeats—I developed a methodology that finally clicked. I noticed that just as my joints needed the right amount of space—not too much, and not too little—to function optimally, the same principle applied to every dimension of life. The Synovial Space™ methodology emerged organically from this intersection of personal challenge and professional insight.

I learned that, just as the synovial spaces between our joints determine physical mobility, life's challenges often create similar spaces—areas that initially feel like limitations but enable new forms of movement if we are attuned to the potential.

Key insight: Limitations are not walls but doorways to unexpected potential.

This insight evolved into a comprehensive approach to creating movement in any area of life. Rather than fighting against limitations, I began to work with them, discovering how they could actually reveal unique pathways forward. The Synovial Space methodology you'll discover in this book is the result of this journey—a practical framework for transforming restrictions into possibilities.

THE SYNOVIAL SPACE DIFFERENCE: WHY THIS APPROACH WORKS

While many personal development methodologies offer valuable insights, the Synovial Space approach differs fundamentally in both philosophy and implementation. Unlike traditional "wheel of life" or "balance" frameworks that often treat life dimensions as separate categories requiring equal attention, this methodology recognizes the following:

1. **Restriction contains wisdom:** Rather than viewing limitations as problems to overcome, this approach recognizes that restrictions often contain the seeds of your greatest contributions. Just as physical limitations can develop specialized abilities, your life challenges hold unique gifts when approached with curiosity rather than resistance.
2. **Systems over segments:** Your life isn't a collection of separate categories but an integrated system where movement in one area creates ripple effects throughout all others. Like the body's joint system, improvement in any dimension enhances the whole rather than just balancing independent parts.
3. **Sustainable over spectacular:** Instead of pursuing dramatic transformations that rarely last, this methodology creates the conditions for natural, sustainable movement. By focusing on creating appropriate space rather than forcing change, you develop momentum that builds over time, rather than having bursts that fade quickly.
4. **Progressive implementation:** Unlike approaches that overwhelm with comprehensive changes, this system guides you through deliberate, sequential development that you control. By starting with your most significant restriction points and gradually expanding, you create lasting change without system overload.
5. **Recovery as essential:** While many frameworks focus exclusively on achievement, this methodology recognizes recovery as fundamental to sustainable growth. Like the necessary

restoration periods in physical training, strategic recovery creates the foundation for all meaningful development.

6. **Personalized pathways:** Rather than prescribing universal solutions, this approach helps you identify your unique starting points, restriction patterns, and movement potential. The frameworks provide structure while honoring your individual circumstances and authentic expression.

The Synovial Space methodology integrates multiple professional disciplines, therapeutic modalities, management expertise, and authentic life experience into a comprehensive transformation system. While traditional personal development approaches offer valuable insights, they often lack the multidimensional perspective that comes from navigating physical limitations, managing diverse teams, and practicing across regulated therapeutic disciplines. This methodology doesn't reject established frameworks; it expands upon them by incorporating proven techniques from multiple disciplines, all validated through measurable outcomes rather than adherence to a single theoretical approach. The result is a uniquely integrated system that addresses the full spectrum of human potential and limitation.

As you progress through this book, you'll discover that this isn't just another life assessment tool but a comprehensive methodology for creating sustainable movement in even the most restricted areas of your life. The journey may be different from what you've experienced with other approaches—more nuanced, more integrated, and ultimately more aligned with how natural systems actually create transformative change.

The Eight Pillars of Dynamic Living

As I began to study the synovial spaces that enable joint movement in our bodies, I noticed a profound parallel: The same principles of creating appropriate space for movement apply to every dimension of our lives. This insight led me to identify eight essential spaces, or pillars, we must maintain for optimal movement in life. Like the synovial spaces in our body which work in harmony to enable fluid motion, these eight pillars create a framework for dynamic living.

1. **Physical space:** Understanding how physical limitations become catalysts for innovative movement.
2. **Mental space:** Creating room for new thoughts when circumstances feel constraining.
3. **Emotional space:** Developing the right balance between connection and independence.
4. **Spiritual space:** Finding purpose, not despite limitations but through them.
5. **Professional space:** Building a career that balance stability and flexibility.
6. **Relational space:** Creating relationships that enable growth without losing connection.
7. **Financial space:** Developing sustainable resource patterns that support your purpose.
8. **Purpose space:** Allowing your unique contribution to emerge and express itself.

These eight pillars don't exist in isolation—they form an interconnected system where movement in one area creates possibility in others. Throughout this book, you'll discover how to identify which pillars need attention in your life, how they affect each other, and how to create the optimal space for movement in each dimension.

Practical Application

Take a moment to rate your current satisfaction with each pillar on a scale of one to ten.

- Physical space:
- Mental space:
- Emotional space:
- Spiritual space:
- Professional space:
- Relational space:
- Financial space:
- Purpose space:

Which areas scored lowest? These may be where you're experiencing the most restriction.

Your Investment in Transformation

This is more than a book—it's a journey of reclaiming your movement potential. The strategies you'll discover have been forged through the following:

- Personal survival against extreme challenges
- Intimate understanding of human resilience
- Systematic deconstruction of limitations
- Practical application across diverse life circumstances

A Critical Invitation

Warning: This is not a passive reading experience. The Synovial Space methodology demands the following:

- Radical self-honesty
- Commitment to genuine exploration
- Willingness to redefine your limitations
- Active engagement with your potential

Are you ready for this level of commitment? If not, this may not be the right time for this journey.

The Unshakable Promise

Growing up in pregentrified Williamsburg, Brooklyn, I learned that resilience is not about avoiding restriction but about creating movement within it. Through this guide, I offer you the same unshakably naive resilience that transformed my life circumstances.

My journey began on the gritty streets of Brooklyn, where survival was an art form learned in the crucible of challenging urban landscapes. From working as a young page at the New York Public Library to navigating the complex worlds of corporate America, hospitality, real estate, and wellness industries, I've transformed obstacles into pathways forward. I've moved from the constraints of 594 Driggs Avenue to bask in nature at the top of my own regenerating acreage estate 780 feet above sea level.

This isn't a tale of accidental success or inherited privilege. It was a systematic application of principles—a deliberate path of personal reinvention. From managing operations in Manhattan's high-end properties to founding a boutique wellness company, from selling real estate in Howard Beach, New York, to cultivating a regenerative mountain home, each step has been an intentional act of growth.

The journey I'll share is not theoretical. These are battle-tested strategies that have been forged through real-world challenges and learned in diverse arenas: corporate boardrooms, airport spas, real estate negotiations, and moments of profound personal reflection. I've transitioned from confined, poverty-stricken urban spaces to an expansive landscape where multiple gullies bear witness to transformation.

This book is an invitation to see your constraints as temporary, your potential as limitless, and your journey as a continuous act of intentional creation. This book and the principles I'll share within are more than a guide; they're a promise. A promise that movement is possible, even in the most restrictive circumstances. A promise of unshakable resilience.

How to Use This Book

This book operates on a fundamental principle: The most powerful solutions emerge from within, waiting to be discovered through careful, comprehensive self-assessment. The Synovial Space methodology is a transformative approach that goes beyond surface-level problem-solving by helping you uncover the true nature of your limitations—distinguishing between real restrictions and perceived barriers.

Through meticulously designed frameworks, you'll embark on a journey of deep self-exploration, mapping your life's current landscape with unprecedented clarity. This isn't about imposing external solutions but about drawing forth the innate wisdom and potential already residing within you. By thoroughly assessing your life across eight critical pillars, you'll learn to identify your actual starting points, understand the nuanced differences between real and perceived restrictions, and develop precise action steps that will emerge organically from your own inner resources.

These frameworks, assessments, and protocols aren't merely exercises; they're professional-grade tools designed to illuminate the hidden pathways of personal movement. Each chart, question set, and process map serves as a key to unlock the solutions that already exist within your unique life experience.

The methodology is specifically crafted for self-motivated individuals who are committed to creating meaningful change. Its meticulously designed tools provide actionable, step-by-step guidance for those who are ready to become the architects of their own transformation. While offering a comprehensive system for independent exploration, the depth of the approach also provides a robust foundation for those seeking additional support or professional guidance.

The true power of this system emerges through a profound dialogue—with yourself through deep reflection, with trusted partners, or with a guide who can help you navigate the intricate landscapes of your potential. The questions posed throughout are more than prompts; they are carefully designed invitations to excavate the solutions waiting to be uncovered within you.

This isn't a book to race through. Each framework deserves space to breathe, to be tested in real conditions, and to reveal its unique application to your circumstances. Approach these tools with both precision and patience, understanding that the most revolutionary solutions are often hidden in the spaces we've yet to fully explore.

As you work through this book, you'll encounter numerous practices, exercises, and action steps across all eight pillars. These are presented comprehensively to provide a complete methodology, but they're not meant to be implemented all at once. Begin by identifying one to three key areas based on your initial assessment, and focus on those practices first. Consistent applying even a few well-chosen exercises will create more meaningful movement than sporadically attempting everything. Remember that this is a journey of progressive development—build your practice systematically rather than rushing to implement every suggestion simultaneously. The frameworks are designed to be revisited as you grow, allowing you to gradually incorporate additional practices when you're ready.

Success Map Exercise

Before we begin, take a moment to visualize.

- Where are you now on your journey?
- What specific restrictions are you facing?
- What would freedom of movement look like for you?
- What small step could you take today toward that vision?

Your Transformation Begins Now

Whether you choose perpetual stagnation or strategic movement, by the end of this guide, you'll experience the following:

- Understand exactly where you are
- Recognize where you could possibly go
- Possess a solid framework to enable your unique movement potential
- Have practical tools for immediate implementation

The synovial space isn't a randomly chosen metaphor; it's a living example of how nature creates movement within apparent restrictions. When you understand that every joint in your body maintains its movement through carefully regulated space, you begin to see how this same principle applies to every area of life.

Are you ready to unlock the movement waiting within you?

Your journey of transformation starts now.

ONE

UNDERSTANDING YOUR SPACE

THE ARCHITECTURE OF SUSTAINABLE GROWTH

Who This Chapter Is For

- Individuals feeling trapped by life circumstances
- Professionals navigating complex personal challenges
- Leaders seeking to understand systemic limitations
- Anyone ready to transform restriction into possibility

Key Transformational Outcomes

By the end of this chapter, you will be able to do the following:

- Understand the nature of personal restrictions
- Recognize how limitations create unexpected opportunities
- Develop a new perspective on movement and potential
- Learn to see challenges as catalysts for growth
- Create a personalized restriction mapping system

The Crucible of Limitation: A Personal Narrative

The synovial spaces in my joints had been shrinking since childhood, but it was the violent encounters of my youth that taught me how fragile the human body could be. By twelve, my osteoarthritis already plagued my movements, though I didn't have a name for it then. One night, a gang assault added new layers of physical memory to my joints, ones that would echo alongside the arthritis for years to come.

What started as a usual Friday-night sleepover at a friend's house transitioned into a late-night rendezvous at a house party. The party was filled with kids I knew well; they happened to be gang-affiliated. The notion of being in a gang repulsed me, but I was already at the party so I went with the flow to appease my close friends.

These early experiences with physical limitation and violence weren't simply traumatic events to overcome—they became the laboratory where I first began to understand how restrictions can para-doxically create new possibilities. While I wouldn't wish these challenges on anyone, they revealed fundamental truths about movement that formed the foundation of the methodology we'll explore throughout this book. The following sections will help you translate these insights into practical approaches for your own journey.

Reflection Point

What unexpected experiences have shaped your understanding of limitation?

How have physical or emotional challenges defined your movement?

When have you found yourself in circumstances you didn't choose but had to navigate?

The Anatomy of Restriction

As we walked through the neighborhood after the party, I kept my distance from the gang members. I was taken off guard by the fact that the neighborhood we were walking through was home to archrivals of these gang members. Seemingly out of nowhere, the nighttime serenity erupted as a mob of eighty-plus gang members descended.

The Visibility Factor

The scene was blurry because I had poor vision (20/200) and wasn't wearing my glasses. The only pair I had were cheap welfare glasses, broken at the nosepiece, which tore into my nose whenever I wore them. It was better to walk around partially blind than to endure constant verbal bullying. Because I couldn't see well, I walked right into the opposing gang members.

Key insight: Sometimes, our greatest vulnerabilities become unexpected teachers, forcing us to develop capabilities we might otherwise never discover.

The Moment of Impact

Surrounded by antagonistic gang members, I felt a stunning blow as one punched me in the face while another crashed a glass bottle over my head. Frozen in shock, I uttered four dumbfounded words: "Is this a joke?"

Despite the weight of the circumstances, I stood my ground, firm on my feet as the mass of thugs pummeled me. I thought they would stop hitting me eventually, but they never did. Instead, one of them tripped me to the ground, and my body became the sounding board for their insecurities.

The Systematic Response

Hobbling home, bloody and beaten, I tried flagging down a police officer patrolling on foot. As I began asking him for help, he yelled at me and said he was going to "kick my ass worse than I already was if I didn't get out of his face." So much for taking an oath to protect and serve.

When I finally made it home, hope for care dissolved quickly. There would be no hospitalization that night. Not because my injuries weren't severe, but because addiction had stripped away the most fundamental maternal instinct: the drive to protect and heal a suffering child. My mother, consumed by exhaustion and the relentless undertow of her substance dependence at the time, dismissed my pain with a curt "too late to go to the ER," her words sharp with a mixture of resignation and indifference.

In that moment of absolute abandonment, something extraordinary took root. Where another might have been crushed, I discovered resilience—not as the absence of pain but as the capacity to create movement within it. My body might have been injured, my care withheld, but my spirit remained unbroken, unbound, and persistently naive in its belief that possibility exists even in the most constricting of spaces.

This was my first masterclass in what would become the core of my life's work: Transformation is not about the circumstances that contain you but about the internal movement you choose to create. Each wave of pain, each moment of neglect, became a chisel sculpting an understanding that limitations are not walls but doorways to unexpected potential.

Restriction Mapping Exercise

Take a moment to identify your own "gang assaults," the moments when systems, circumstances, or people created profound restriction.

1. **Physical Restrictions**

- What bodily limitations affect your daily movement?
- How have these shaped your approach to challenges?
- What adaptations have you developed?

2. **System Failures**

- When have support systems failed you?
- What institutions have proved inadequate?
- How did you navigate without proper support?

3. **Internal Beliefs**

- What stories about yourself feel permanent?
- Which beliefs came from past trauma?
- What protection mechanisms are now holding you back?

When faced with limitation, most of us instinctively push against it, fighting for our original vision of movement. Yet what I discovered through both my osteoarthritis and the aftermath of violence was something counterintuitive: Sometimes, the most powerful movement comes not from fighting against restrictions but from working with them to discover new pathways.

The Unexpected Gift: Finding Movement in Restriction

If there was physical, mental, or social therapy available to me then, I was unaware of it. Instead, I was forced to internalize my trauma and dismantle the built-up anxieties of this and many other negative life events. This necessity for self-reliance became an unexpected teacher.

Coaching Moment: Systems and Solutions

That night taught me something crucial about restrictions: They rarely come with warning signs. Whether it's a sudden physical assault or a gradual diagnosis like osteoarthritis, life has a way of throwing limitations at us when we least expect them. But here's what I've learned: It's not the restriction that defines us but how we create or undermine movement within the space we're given.

Unconventional Resources

Instead of seeking professional therapy as a youth, I worked through my internal battles by reading war novels such as *All Quiet on the Western Front*. Reading stories of people who had survived harrowing experiences far worse than my own was deeply enlightening. I paid close attention to how soldiers had reacted to negative experiences during quiet moments on the front lines.

The personal resource inventory below is a powerful self-reflection tool designed to uncover the hidden sources of strength that have guided you through life's most challenging moments. By mapping out your unconventional resources, you'll gain a deeper understanding of your resilience, creativity, and inner capacity to overcome obstacles.

Why is this exercise so crucial? Our most transformative support often comes from unexpected places: books that spoke to our souls, mentors who appeared at critical moments, personal practices that sustained us, or community connections that provided unexpected comfort. Many of these resources go unrecognized, yet they are the invisible scaffolding that has supported our personal growth.

As you complete this inventory, you'll do the following:

- Recognize the diverse ways you've found strength
- Appreciate the unique pathways of your personal healing
- Identify patterns of resilience you may have overlooked
- Develop a comprehensive view of your emotional survival tool kit

This isn't just an inventory—it's a celebration of your journey and a testament to your ability to find light in unexpected places.

Personal Resource Inventory
What unconventional resources have helped you through difficult times?

Resource Type	Examples from Your Life	How It Helped
Books/Media		
Unexpected Mentors		
Personal Practices		
Community Connections		
Inner Strengths		

Finding Your Synovial Space

Physical pain has a way of teaching us about boundaries. My osteoarthritis forced me to understand the precise internal spaces where movement was possible. We each have systems we can assimilate and align into our life that help propel us forward. By consistently adding systems to our tool kit, we fortify our overall system (our life).

Mapping Your Restricted Spaces

Just as a manual therapist should assess joint mobility before creating a treatment plan, we need to understand our current limitations before designing growth strategies. This mapping process requires honest evaluation without judgment—seeing restrictions as valuable data rather than personal failings.

Begin by identifying where movement feels limited across all eight pillars, noting both obvious blockages and subtle resistance points. Pay particular attention to areas where you've repeatedly attempted change without success, as these often indicate systematic patterns rather than simple motivation issues.

Like a skilled clinician differentiating between joint capsule tightness and muscular tension, learn to distinguish between external circumstances and internal response patterns. This precise assessment creates the foundation for effective strategies, allowing you to address recurring patterns rather than isolated symptoms, and to create space where it will generate the most significant movement across your entire system.

Comprehensive Space Audit
Rate each dimension on a scale of 1–10.
(1 = completely restricted, 10 = optimal movement)

Life Dimension	Current Rating	Key Restrictions	Available Movement	Potential Next Step
Physical Space				
Mental Space				
Emotional Space				
Spiritual Space				
Professional Space				
Relational Space				
Financial Space				
Purpose Space				

The Financial Movement Connection

Physical restrictions taught me that financial movement is more about creating the right amount of space for sustainable progress than it is about creating dramatic, rapid progress. Just as joints require precise space to function optimally, our financial lives can benefit from the right balance of structure and flexibility.

Financial Movement Assessment

- Where do you feel most financially restricted?
- What small adjustments might create new financial space?
- How could more flexibility in one financial area create movement in others?
- What one small financial habit could create significant long-term space?

Understanding how to find movement within restriction is the first step. Now let's translate this understanding into practical action that creates sustainable change in your life.

Action Planning: Your Next Movement

Just as manual therapy requires small, consistent movements to create lasting change, personal growth happens in carefully chosen steps. As I learned new manual therapy modalities that worked with my osteoarthritis rather than against it, the investment paid for itself by affording me more access to body control and slowing my degradation.

Key Implementation Tool: This framework transforms insights into structured action. While the other exercises in this chapter help you understand your current situation, this plan creates your path forward. At this stage, focus on identifying your starting point and your next movement rather than planning the entire ninety days in detail. You'll refine this plan as you progress through the book.

Ninety-Day Movement Action Plan

1. **Identify Your Starting Point**

- Select the pillar showing most resistance or causing greatest limitation in your life.
- Honestly assess your current capabilities and restrictions within this area.
- Inventory existing resources, relationships, and tools already available to you.

2. **Define Your Next Movement**

- Choose one minimal action that creates immediate space without overwhelming your system.
- Connect this new action to existing daily habits that will naturally prompt you to perform it.
- Identify specific people, environments, or tools that will reinforce this new movement

3. **Create an Implementation Timeline**

- Schedule two- to five-minute daily practices that build the foundation for larger change.
- Establish a consistent day and time to evaluate progress and make adjustments.
- **Thirty-day assessment point:** Schedule time to reflect on changes in how this area feels, noting new movements that have become possible.
- **Ninety-day expansion goal:** Envision how continued space creation in this area might transform your overall movement potential.

Building Your Support System

Growing up, I found solace in reading war novels and stories about soldiers who supported each other through impossible situations. I learned that personal growth rarely happens in isolation. We all need our own tribe—people who understand our restrictions and support our movement.

Understanding your support system is more than a passive inventory—it's an active blueprint for personal transformation. Just as soldiers rely on their unit for survival, we, too, must intentionally cultivate networks that sustain, challenge, and elevate us. The Connection Mapping Exercise is your strategic approach to building a resilient, dynamic support system that can adapt and grow with your evolving needs.

Think of this map not as a static document but as a living, breathing network of potential—a road map to deliberately design the support structures that will propel you forward. By identifying your current resources, recognizing gaps, and planning deliberate next steps, you'll transform connection from a passive experience to an intentional strategy of personal growth.

Connection Mapping Exercise

Support Type	Current Resources	Gaps to Fill	Next Connection Step
Physical Support			
Emotional Support			
Mental/Knowledge			
Spiritual Guidance			
Professional Growth			
Financial Wisdom			

Chapter Integration: Your Movement Architecture

These early experiences with restriction—from my father's absence to my physical limitations and financial constraints—didn't just shape my understanding of movement; they laid the foundation for what I would later conceptualize as the eight pillars of movement. Each challenge revealed how restriction in one area inevitably affects all others, but also how creating space in any dimension can open new possibilities across our entire life architecture.

Understanding the Eight Pillars of Dynamic Living

Just as our joints require synovial fluid to move freely, every dimension of our lives needs the right amount of space to function optimally. The Synovial Space methodology identifies eight interconnected pillars that, together, create the complete architecture of human movement and potential.

The Eight Pillars Defined

1. **Physical pillar:** Your body's capacity for movement, energy, and vitality. This encompasses not just fitness but how physical space and sensation inform all other life dimensions.
2. **Mental pillar:** Your cognitive clarity, focus, and ability to process information. This includes decision-making capacity, problem-solving ability, and mental flexibility.
3. **Emotional pillar:** Your capacity to feel, process, and express the full spectrum of human emotions without becoming overwhelmed or disconnected.
4. **Spiritual pillar:** Your connection to something greater than yourself—whether through faith, nature, purpose, or philosophical understanding—that provides meaning and direction.
5. **Professional pillar:** Your ability to create value, express talents, and contribute meaningfully through your work, regardless of its form.
6. **Relational pillar:** Your capacity for authentic connection with others, from intimate relationships to professional networks and community bonds.
7. **Financial pillar:** Your relationship with resources and abundance, encompassing both practical money management and deeper beliefs about value and worth.
8. **Purpose pillar:** Your authentic expression and unique contribution to the world—the intersection where your deepest gifts meet the world's needs.

The Interconnected System

These pillars don't exist in isolation. Like the fasciae that connect every part of your physical body, each pillar influences and is influenced by all others. A restriction in one area inevitably creates compensatory patterns throughout the entire system. Conversely, creating movement in any single pillar can catalyze transformation across all dimensions.

Consider how financial stress (financial pillar) affects sleep quality (physical), which impacts cognitive function (mental), strains relationships (relational), and clouds sense of purpose (purpose).

This interconnection means that sustainable transformation requires a systematic approach, addressing not just symptoms but the entire architecture of restriction and movement.

The Methodology: From Restriction to Movement

The Synovial Space approach follows a natural progression that mirrors how our bodies heal and adapt.

1. **Recognition:** Identifying where restriction exists across all eight pillars, and understanding that these limitations often contain the seeds of your greatest potential.
2. **Assessment:** Comprehensively evaluating your current range of motion in each dimension, mapping both restrictions and existing capacities.
3. **Narrative revision:** Examining and rewriting the stories that create your movement patterns, transforming limiting beliefs into empowering possibilities.
4. **Strategic movement:** Creating intentional, sustainable movement starting from your edges, where growth is possible without overwhelming the system.
5. **Integration:** Developing practices that maintain optimal space across all pillars, preventing future restrictions while supporting continued expansion.
6. **Recovery:** Understanding that rest and integration are not optional but essential components of sustainable growth and performance.

Your Journey Through This Book

Each chapter builds upon this framework, providing both understanding and practical tools.

Chapter 2 guides you through comprehensive assessment across all eight pillars.

Chapter 3 teaches you to identify and rewrite limiting narratives.

Chapter 4 shows you how to find and safely expand your edges.

Chapter 5 demonstrates how to create sustainable movement patterns.

Chapter 6 reveals the critical role of recovery in maintaining progress.

Chapter 7 brings it all together through a detailed case study.

The appendix extends the methodology to collective transformation.

The Promise of This Approach

Unlike traditional self-improvement methods that focus on forcing change in isolated areas, the Synovial Space methodology works with your body's natural wisdom. By creating the right amount of space—not too much, and not too little—in each dimension of life, you enable movement that is both sustainable and transformative.

This isn't about becoming someone different. It's about creating the conditions that allow your authentic self to move freely in the world. Whether you're facing a specific life challenge, seeking to optimize your performance, or simply sensing that more is possible, this framework provides a path from wherever you are to wherever you're meant to be.

The restrictions you'll identify aren't failures—they're the precise starting points for your unique journey of transformation. Every limitation contains information about what wants to move, and every movement creates new possibilities across your entire life system.

As you continue through this chapter and into the comprehensive assessment that follows, *remember*: You're not broken, and you don't need fixing. You're a dynamic system capable of extraordinary movement once you understand how to create and maintain the space you need to thrive.

Key Chapter Takeaways

1. Restrictions are not end points but starting points for new movement.
2. Systems often fail us, requiring personal adaptation and growth.
3. Unconventional resources can provide unexpected support.
4. True assessment must precede meaningful action.
5. Small, consistent movements create sustainable change.
6. Support systems are essential for optimal growth.

Your Immediate Next Steps

1. Complete the Restriction Mapping Exercise.
2. Conduct your Comprehensive Space Audit.
3. Identify one small action to take within twenty-four hours.

Just as understanding joint movement begins with assessing mobility at the articular level, we must thoroughly evaluate all dimensions of our lives before creating effective action plans. This comprehensive assessment provides the foundation for meaningful forward progress.

The journey we've begun in this chapter lays the foundation for everything that follows. By understanding your current restrictions and recognizing them as potential pathways for growth, you've taken the first step toward creating authentic movement in your life. The exercises you've completed aren't just reflective tools—they're the beginning of a practical road map for transformation.

The next chapter will guide you through this vital assessment process, helping you map your current range of motion across all life dimensions. We'll create a clearer picture of your starting point—not to highlight limitations but to understand exactly where and how to create new movement possibilities.

Commitment moment: What one small movement will you make in the next twenty-four hours to create space in your most restricted area?

TWO

ASSESSING YOUR SPACES

MAPPING YOUR MOVEMENT POTENTIAL

Who This Chapter Is For

- Professionals seeking comprehensive self-understanding
- Individuals ready for holistic personal assessment
- Leaders looking to unlock hidden potential
- Anyone committed to evidence-based personal growth

Key Transformational Outcomes

By the end of this chapter, you will be able to do the following:

- Develop a comprehensive personal assessment framework
- Understand the interconnections between life dimensions
- Create a precise map of your current movement potential
- Transform assessment insights into actionable growth strategies
- Build sustainable tracking systems for ongoing development

THE ORIGIN OF ASSESSMENT: A PERSONAL JOURNEY OF DISCOVERY

My first official osteoarthritis diagnosis came inadvertently during a follow-up with my primary doctor after a grueling bout with kidney stones in my early twenties. A nagging symptom of inner groin pain had spread to my outer hips. Our findings resulted in a referral to a rheumatologist, which led to a path of several more tests and culminated with a positive diagnosis of stage two osteoarthritis in both hips and signs of stage two degradation in the coccyx, and sacroiliac.

Reflection Point

What unexpected health challenges have revealed deeper truths about your capabilities?

When has a limitation in one area exposed connections to other life dimensions?

How have diagnostic experiences shaped your understanding of yourself?

The Assessment Moment: A Blueprint Emerges

The rheumatologist's assessment was methodical and revealing. They performed end-range and sensory stimulation tests. For the end-range tests, they moved my limbs until they saw compensations or I reached a normal end range. The sensory stimulation tests showed the neural drive for each muscle.

They tested my internal isometric strength to see if any tendons were injured. That assessment was the start of my interest in learning my biomechanical abilities and limitations.

Key insight: Assessment is not about judgment but about creating a precise map of your current reality that allows for intentional movement.

THE ARCHITECTURE OF COMPREHENSIVE ASSESSMENT

These moments in my life sparked my interest in learning more about my architecture—what I had to work with, what was truly restricted, and what possibilities remained. I could start to tie together which tendon had fibrosis around it, and what I could do about it: Train positional isometrics from low intensity up the chain.

But what could I possibly train before assessing what I was training for? Assessment is where real change begins—not with hopes, dreams, or determination but with honest evaluation.

The assessment process you're about to undertake follows a clear progression: First, we'll evaluate each pillar individually to understand specific areas of restriction and possibility. Then, we'll examine how these pillars interact as an integrated system. Finally, we'll develop a personalized assessment rhythm that creates sustainable awareness. This systematic approach ensures you'll gain both specific insights and a holistic understanding of your movement potential.

Assessment principle: Like an architect examining a building's foundation before any renovation can begin, you need to understand your system's structure before adding linear loads, ignoring the fascial underbelly weaving between, as, and part of the system.

Common Assessment Pitfalls

This need for accurate assessment reflects challenges many face in their personal growth journeys.

- **The enthusiasm trap:** Repeatedly attempting fitness programs without understanding physical starting points, leading to injuries or plateaus.

- **The prestige pursuit:** Chasing career advancement without assessing true strengths and values, creating internal misalignment.

- **The cookie-cutter fallacy:** Developing financial strategies based on generic advice rather than evaluating unique situations.

All these patterns share one feature: They attempt to build solutions without first understanding the foundation they're building upon.

Creating Your Assessment Architecture

Just as my rheumatologist established baseline measurements to track progress, regular assessment across all life dimensions creates a foundation for meaningful change.

Strategic Assessment Schedule

Frequency	Focus Areas	Time Investment	Documentation Method
Daily	Quick body scans and mood checks	3–5 minutes	Journal/app notes
Weekly	Deeper check-ins across all pillars	15–30 minutes	Structured review
Monthly	Comprehensive assessment and pattern recognition	1–2 hours	Full evaluation
Quarterly	Major progress evaluation and direction adjustment	2–4 hours	Strategic planning

Assessment guidance: As you work through each pillar assessment, pay attention to patterns that emerge across different areas of your life. Note which pillars feel most restricted and which offer the most natural movement. These patterns will guide your prioritization in later chapters. Complete all eight assessments before moving to the pillar connection mapping, as understanding each dimension individually will prepare you for seeing their relationships.

THE EIGHT PILLARS ASSESSMENT FRAMEWORK

My rheumatologist's methodical assessment provided a powerful model for personal transformation. Just as they evaluated each joint's mobility before developing a treatment plan, we must examine all dimensions of our lives with the same precision. Each pillar requires thorough evaluation before we can create meaningful change.

1. Physical Pillar: The Architecture of Movement

I've included this comprehensive joint mobility assessment for those interested in learning more about their physical movement capabilities through the lens of their synovial spaces. Don't get bogged down by the terminology or precise degrees of motion—this is simply a template showing average ranges where most human bodies typically function optimally. Everyone's body is unique, and your personal "normal" may differ based on your history and structure.

Sometimes, having a general understanding is the most valuable starting point. For those able to complete this framework either independently or with assistance from a movement professional, it will serve as an excellent baseline to track your mobility over time. You can return to this assessment periodically to document progress in your restriction points and celebrate improvements in your movement capacity.

The goal isn't to achieve perfect scores but to develop awareness of your current physical reality—the foundation for creating intentional movement in all dimensions of your life.

Current Active Range Assessment

Use this framework to map your joint mobility using this simple tracking system.

Joint	Movement Direction	Current Range	Normal Range	Restriction Level (1–10)	Compensation Patterns
Neck	Forward Flexion		45–50°		
	Extension		55–70°		
	Left Rotation		70–80°		
	Right Rotation		70–80°		
Shoulders	Flexion (L/R)		165–180°		
	Extension (L/R)		50–60°		
	Internal Rotation (L/R)		60–70°		
	External Rotation (L/R)		80–90°		
Wrists	Flexion (L/R)		80–90°		
	Extension (L/R)		70–80°		
	Internal Rotation (L/R)		30–40°		
	External Rotation (L/R)		15–20°		
Forearms	Internal Rotation (L/R)		80–90°		
	External Rotation (L/R)		80–90°		
Elbows	Flexion (L/R)		135–150°		
	Extension (L/R)		0–10°		
Spine	Flexion		60–80°		
	Extension		20–30°		
	Lateral Flexion (L/R)		25–35°		
	Rotation (L/R)		30–45°		
Hips	Flexion (L/R)		110–120°		
	Extension (L/R)		10–20°		
	Internal Rotation (L/R)		30–40°		
	External Rotation (L/R)		40–50°		

Joint	Movement Direction	Current Range	Normal Range	Restriction Level (1–10)	Compensation Patterns
Knees	Flexion (L/R)		130–150°		
	Extension (L/R)		0–5°		
	Internal Rotation (L/R)		20–30°		
	External Rotation (L/R)		30–40°		
Ankles	Dorsiflexion (L/R)		15–20°		
	Plantarflexion (L/R)		45–50°		
	Internal Rotation (L/R)		30–35°		
	External Rotation (L/R)		15–20°		

Assessment Guidance

As you complete this assessment, perform each movement slowly and mindfully, stopping at the point where you feel resistance—not pain. Again, the goal isn't to achieve perfect scores but to develop awareness of your current physical reality. Notice which movements feel restricted versus which flow naturally, and pay particular attention to compensation patterns—how other body parts might be moving to accommodate limitations.

This physical mapping serves two essential purposes: First, it begins to create concrete awareness of your current movement capacity, directly revealing the gap between how you currently move and how you need to move based on both your present lifestyle and desired future activities. Second, it develops the internal sensitivity needed to recognize subtle signals throughout all life dimensions.

Note on assessment scope: This framework focuses on the major synovial joints that most significantly impact daily movement and physical capacity. For a more comprehensive assessment, you might also evaluate the temporomandibular joint (jaw), fingers, and toes if these areas are particularly relevant to your specific activities or concerns. The principles of assessment remain the same—look for restrictions in range, quality of control, and compensation patterns.

Movement Control Assessment
Rate your active range and movement quality for each joint on a scale of 1–10.
(1 = highly restricted, 10 = optimal control)

- Ability to move slowly and deliberately:
- Capacity to start and stop movements:
- Stability through available ranges:
- Response to fatigue:
- Breathing integration:

For a more comprehensive understanding, consider seeking assistance from a qualified practitioner (physical therapist, chiropractor, or movement specialist) to assess both active and passive ranges of motion. Passive range—how far a joint can move when externally assisted—should ideally be about 10 percent greater than your active range. This relationship between active and passive mobility provides crucial insight into your neuromuscular control, highlighting whether limitations stem from structural issues or motor control patterns that can be addressed through targeted practice.

Just as joint limitations restrict physical movement, constraints in other pillars similarly affect life capacity. By practicing this precise observation with your physical body—the most tangible pillar—you're developing the awareness skills needed to accurately assess the less visible dimensions we'll explore next.

2. Mental Pillar: The Architecture of Thought

When I was that kid getting jumped by gang members, my blurred vision from not wearing glasses forced an immediate adaptation. There was no conscious decision to rely on my other senses—my body and mind simply responded in the moment. My words ("Is this a joke?") revealed how shock can override calculated thought in crisis. Even as I stood my ground, I was dumbfounded by my own response. These instinctive reactions to extreme circumstances shape our mental patterns, creating their own architecture of possibility and limitation.

It's precisely because our automatic responses emerge without conscious thought that deliberate self-assessment becomes crucial. Fight-or-flight reactions serve us in moments of crisis but can solidify into limiting patterns when left unexamined. By methodically assessing these patterns across all eight pillars, we create the opportunity for intentional evolution rather than remaining bound by unconscious adaptations. This progressive movement toward positive growth begins with understanding our current automatic responses before we can transform them.

Mental Assessment Framework
Thought Pattern Tracking

Pattern Type	Examples in Your Life	Impact (1–10)	Change Potential
Limiting Beliefs			
Thought Loops			
Decision Frameworks			
Learning Methods			
Problem-Solving Approaches			

Key Questions

- How do your thought patterns influence your daily movements?
- Where do you find clarity versus confusion in your thinking?
- What mental adaptations have you developed through challenges?
- How do you process and respond to unexpected situations?
- What thinking patterns serve your growth, and which limit it?

Just as your thoughts shape your experiences, your emotions color your perceptions and drive your actions. Let's explore how your emotional landscape influences your capacity for authentic movement.

3. Emotional Pillar: The Architecture of Feeling

That early assault by gang members, and the policeman's subsequent dismissal of my need for help, taught me that emotional assessment requires both honesty and precision. Understanding our emotional architecture means recognizing both our responses and our resilience.

In the context of creating sustainable movement, a trigger refers to a specific cue or prompt that automatically initiates your space creation practices. Unlike negative triggers that might provoke unwanted reactions, implementation triggers are intentionally designed to serve as positive cues that activate beneficial behaviors. These triggers create reliable pathways for consistent practice by connecting new habits to existing patterns in your life.

For example, you might use your first sip of morning coffee as a trigger for a thirty-second breathing practice, or use the sound of your phone notification as a reminder to mobilize during long bouts of repetitive or sedentary tasks. By linking space creation practices to these established cues, you reduce the need for willpower and create more automatic implementation.

Emotional Intelligence Mapping

It's important to understand that emotional trigger situations are specific circumstances, interactions, or environments that consistently evoke particular emotional responses in you. Unlike implementation triggers (briefly mentioned above; positive cues for beneficial habits), emotional triggers often operate below conscious awareness, automatically activating emotional patterns before you've had time to choose your response.

These triggers might include certain types of interactions (like receiving criticism), specific environments (such as crowded spaces), particular relationships, or even subtle cues like specific tones of voice or body language. By mapping these trigger situations alongside your physical responses and coping mechanisms, you'll develop greater awareness of your emotional patterns and create more space for intentional responses rather than automatic reactions.

Before completing this framework, take a moment to reflect on your emotional patterns without judgment. The goal isn't to eliminate emotions but to understand how they manifest in your life. This assessment helps you identify both your emotional triggers and your typical responses, creating awareness that forms the foundation for future choice. As you map each emotion, consider both recent examples and recurring patterns throughout your life.

Emotional Pattern Identification

Emotion	Trigger Situations	Physical Responses	Typical Duration	Coping Mechanisms
Anger				
Fear				
Joy				
Sadness				
Shame				

Response to Assessment Questions

- How do you typically respond to challenges?
- What emotional patterns emerge in difficult situations?
- Where do you find strength in adversity?
- How do past experiences influence your current responses?
- What emotional resources help you move forward?

While emotions provide the energy for movement, your sense of purpose gives it direction. Let's examine how your connection to deeper meaning shapes your movement potential.

4. Spiritual Pillar: The Architecture of Purpose

During the gang assault, hearing myself utter those four dumbfounded words ("Is this a joke?") while standing my ground revealed something profound about inner strength and purpose. Much like a physical assessment maps our body's capabilities, we must understand how our deeper beliefs and values guide our movements through life.

In that moment of crisis, my response wasn't calculated—it emerged from something deeper than conscious thought. When stripped of time to deliberate, our core values and instinctive beliefs reveal themselves through our actions. Standing my ground despite overwhelming odds showed me that courage wasn't something I needed to develop—it was already there, waiting to emerge when needed. These glimpses of our authentic nature during extreme circumstances provide invaluable insights into who we truly are beneath our carefully constructed identities. They offer a window into the beliefs and values that actually drive our movements, not just the ones we intellectually claim to hold.

My own spiritual journey has been far from linear. Like many, I've moved through different phases of belief—from my Catholic upbringing to a period of passionate evangelism when I performed Christian rap and contemplated becoming a youth pastor. Yet it was my deepest questions, not my certainties, that ultimately created the most space for authentic growth.

I found myself wrestling with foundational concepts, questioning narratives I had accepted without examination, and struggling to reconcile theological teachings with my lived experiences. These weren't casual doubts but profound confrontations with my core understanding of meaning and purpose. Each question created both discomfort and possibility—restriction and space—simultaneously.

What I discovered through this ongoing journey was something unexpected: Spiritual movement doesn't always mean arriving at perfect answers. Sometimes, it means developing the capacity to hold questions with courage. My most significant spiritual growth came not from resolving all contradictions but from learning to navigate life with authenticity despite them.

This pattern—finding movement within spiritual questions rather than requiring absolute certainty —became a foundational principle in my approach to purpose. Many of us restrict our spiritual movement by believing we must have complete clarity before proceeding. Yet our deepest values often guide us most effectively when we create space for both conviction and questioning, certainty and wonder.

The spiritual assessment that follows isn't about evaluating the "correctness" of your beliefs, but rather understanding how your relationship with meaning and purpose either constrains or enables authentic movement in your life.

Purpose Alignment Assessment

List your top five to seven core values.

A. **For each value, rate the following:**

- **Current expression in daily life (1–10):** Assess how consistently this value is reflected in your regular activities, decisions, and time allocation.

- **Importance to your sense of purpose (1–10):** Evaluate how central this value is to your definition of a meaningful life.

- **Alignment with current life direction (1–10):** Consider how well your current path supports and reinforces this core value.

B. **Meaning Assessment**

- **What activities make you lose track of time?** Identify specific experiences that create a state of flow where your engagement is so complete that time seems to disappear.

- **When do you feel most alive?** Note the circumstances, environments, and actions that create your strongest sense of vitality and presence.

- **What contribution do you feel drawn to make?** Describe the impact you feel naturally motivated to have on others, your community, or the world.

Guiding Questions

- What principles guide your major life decisions?
- How do your core values influence your movement choices?
- Where does your deepest sense of purpose come from?
- How do your beliefs affect your responses to challenges?
- What gives you strength in difficult moments?

Your sense of purpose naturally extends to how you interact with resources. Let's investigate how your financial patterns either restrict or enable movement in your life.

5. Professional Pillar: The Architecture of Impact

When I was managing staff in luxury hotels, residential buildings, and some of the top commercial properties in New York City, asking the right questions of my team opened up new revenue streams, led to productivity gains, and increased customer service scores. Talent management begins from within.

Professional Impact Assessment
Value Creation Mapping

Impact Area	Current Contribution	Potential Growth	Development Needs	Next-Level Vision
Skills				
Knowledge				
Network				
Leadership				
Innovation				

Career Trajectory Analysis

- Where are you (beginning/middle/transition/mastery) on your professional journey?
- What professional patterns have served you well?
- What patterns need evolution?
- Where do you currently create the most value?

Assessment Questions

- How do you create value in your current role?
- Where do you make your most meaningful impact?
- What professional patterns support your growth?
- How do you build capacity in yourself and others?
- Where might your challenges create unexpected strengths?

Your professional and personal lives intersect through your relationships with others. Let's examine how your social connections influence your movement possibilities.

6. Relational Pillar: The Architecture of Connection

Just as we must assess physical movement patterns, we need to understand how we navigate our social connections. Throughout my various roles and life stages, I've discovered that meaningful engagement comes from intentional presence and thoughtful inquiry. My greatest fulfillment has come from asking the right questions at the right time to the right people—but this ability didn't develop by accident. It required first establishing authentic connections and then approaching each interaction with genuine curiosity rather than predetermined agendas.

To understand your own relationship patterns, take time to map your current social ecosystem using the framework below. For each relationship type, identify the key people who populate that space in your life. Then honestly assess both the quality of these connections (how meaningful and authentic they feel) and their reciprocity (the balance of giving and receiving). Finally, note the potential for growth in each area. This mapping creates awareness of both your existing social resources and opportunities for more intentional connection.

Relationship Ecosystem Mapping
Connection Assessment

Relationship Type	Key People	Quality (1–10)	Reciprocity (1–10)	Growth Potential
Family				
Friends				
Mentors				
Colleagues				
Community				

Social Pattern Recognition

- In which social contexts do you feel most authentic?
- Where do you tend to withdraw, and where do you tend to perform?
- What relationship patterns have become limitations?
- Which connections consistently energize you?

Assessment Questions

- How do your relationships support your growth?
- Where do you find genuine connection?
- What social patterns help your movement, and which ones hinder your movement?
- How do you create space for authentic interaction?
- What roles do others play in your development?

Your relationships exist within physical contexts that shape your experience. Let's explore how your environments—both created and natural—affect your capacity for movement.

7. Financial Pillar: The Architecture of Resources

Growing up in poverty under the plague of addiction in Williamsburg, Brooklyn, the notion of receiving care for my pain was as foreign as seeing a sports car pass by my apartment. Just as we assess physical limitations, we must understand how our resources affect our movement through life.

My financial journey began early, working at the New York Public Library at age fourteen while still navigating the challenges of having limited resources at home. What followed was not a straight path to prosperity, but rather a winding road of financial restrictions that taught me profound lessons about creating movement within constraint.

Like many, I experienced the crushing weight of debt—taking on additional financial burdens during an early divorce at nineteen to move forward with my life, even when it seemed financially irrational. I bounced between apartments across New York's boroughs, living paycheck to paycheck while still investing what little I had in my own growth through classes, education, and personal development. This pattern of prioritizing growth even during scarcity would later prove to be a crucial strategy for creating financial movement.

The purchase of our first home in Ozone Park illustrated another critical lesson in financial space creation. Buying just before the real estate bubble collapsed, we found ourselves underwater with both a mortgage and a construction loan on a property that needed more work than we had anticipated. For nine years, we made difficult choices—my wife left her hotel management position to open a family day care in our home to be closer to our daughter, and we accepted a 75 percent income reduction in exchange for something more meaningful than money alone.

During this period, our children slept on mattresses on the floor because furniture was a luxury we couldn't afford. Even with titles like director and general manager on our résumés, we sometimes struggled to buy groceries at the end of the month. These experiences taught me that financial restriction isn't simply about income level—it exists at every tier of apparent success when expenses and obligations compress your available resources.

The turning point came through an unconventional move: downsizing from our house to a one-bedroom apartment. This deliberate financial restriction—counter to the typical "bigger is better" narrative—actually created new space for movement in other areas of our lives. The reduced financial pressure allowed me to pursue acting training and new career directions that had previously seemed impossible.

This pattern of strategic restriction creating unexpected movement continued when we eventually purchased property in California. By applying what we'd learned through years of financial challenges, we approached this investment differently—seeing possibilities rather than just limitations. The result was that we created significant equity that ultimately funded our next evolution.

These experiences shaped my understanding of financial space: It's not about the absolute amount of resources, but how we create movement within whatever constraints exist. Just as a skilled martial artist can generate tremendous power in a restricted space, you can achieve financial well-being not by having unlimited resources but by mastering movement within your current parameters.

Now let's apply these insights to your own financial landscape. The following assessment will help you map your current financial movement patterns and identify opportunities for creating new space. For each category, honestly evaluate your current state, note the level of restriction you feel (with ten being most restricted), identify potential movement opportunities, and determine one specific next step. This isn't about comparing yourself to external standards, but about recognizing where you can create more effective movement within your unique circumstances.

Financial Movement Assessment
Resource Flow Tracking

Resource Category	Current State	Restriction Level (1–10)	Movement Potential	Next Step
Income Streams				
Savings				
Debt Structure				
Investment Growth				
Financial Knowledge				
Resource Network				

Financial Mindset Evaluation

- What money beliefs did you inherit from your upbringing?
- How do you define "enough"?
- What financial fears restrict your movement?
- Where do you feel most empowered financially?

Assessment Questions

- How do your current resources enable or limit your movement?
- What financial patterns have you developed from your experiences?
- Where do you feel most restricted by resources?
- How do you create movement within financial constraints?
- What financial strengths have you developed through necessity?

Just as financial resources provide material support for movement, your professional expression creates impact in the world. Let's explore how your work life shapes your capacity for meaningful action.

8. Purpose Pillar: The Architecture of Meaning

Your sense of purpose—what you're here to contribute, the direction that pulls you forward, and the legacy you're building—represents perhaps the most integrative of all eight pillars. Purpose isn't something you find through endless searching. It reveals itself through living your values, contributing what you can, and paying attention to what creates meaning in your life.

My own journey with purpose followed an unexpected path. My limitations—early-onset osteoarthritis, color vision deficiency, and the physical restrictions that closed certain doors—forced me to ask deeper questions. What if restriction itself could become purpose? What if helping others navigate their constraints could become not just work but my calling?

That reframe changed everything. My purpose isn't something I achieve despite my limitations. It emerges because of how I've learned to work with my limitations. The Synovial Space methodology itself grew from restriction as each physical challenge taught me something about creating movement within constraints that applies across all life dimensions.

Purpose at twenty-five looks different than purpose at forty-five, which looks different than purpose at sixty-five. This isn't failure—it's evolution. As your capacity changes, your contribution changes. As your experience deepens, your meaning-making capacity expands. Purpose isn't a destination you reach. It's a process of continual alignment between your deepest values and how you show up in the world.

Before exploring where you might create more space in your purpose pillar, it's helpful to establish your current baseline. The assessment below isn't about judgment—a low score doesn't mean you lack purpose. It simply reveals where you might feel disconnected, and where that disconnection might be creating unnecessary strain. Answer honestly. This is for you alone.

Purpose Assessment Framework

This assessment helps you evaluate your current sense of purpose and identify where creating more space might unlock greater meaning. Purpose doesn't require a platform, recognition, or dramatic impact. It happens in raising your children with intention, showing up at work with integrity, contributing to your community in small ways, creating beauty where you can, and living in a way that is aligned with your values.

Rate your current experience in each dimension on a scale of 1–10.

(1 = completely disconnected, 10 = deeply aligned)

Direction and Calling

- Sense of your clear direction:
- Connection to what pulls you forward:
- Confidence in your path:

Contribution and Impact

- Sense of meaningful contribution:
- Clarity about how you serve others:
- Feeling that your work matters:

Values Alignment

- Clarity about your core values:
- Alignment between your values and daily life:
- Courage to live by your values:

Legacy and Long-Term Vision

- Clarity about what you're building:
- Connection to something larger than yourself:
- Sense of creating lasting value:

Meaning-Making Capacity

- Ability to find meaning in your daily activities:
- Connection to your purpose during difficulties:
- Sense of your life having significance:

Numbers reveal patterns, but purpose lives in the specifics. The questions below help you move from general assessment to concrete understanding. You don't need to answer every question—let them incite reflection rather than create another obligation. If one question resonates, stay with it. If another feels irrelevant, skip it. You're looking for insight, not completion.

Purpose Reflection Questions

Consider the following questions as you explore your purpose pillar:

- What activities make you lose track of time?
- When do you feel most alive and engaged?
- What problems in the world break your heart?
- What would you do even if no one recognized your effort or paid you for it?
- What do others consistently ask for your help with?
- What do you want to be remembered for?
- Where do your deepest gifts meet the world's needs?

These questions help you identify purpose—what matters, what calls to you, and where meaning lives. But identifying purpose isn't the same as sustaining it. Purpose requires nourishment, especially during seasons of limitation or change. The assessment below evaluates not what you believe about purpose but how you're actively maintaining connection to it. This is where theory becomes practice.

Purpose Recovery Assessment

Just as physical recovery requires specific attention, purpose recovery requires intentional nourishment. This assessment helps you evaluate your practices for maintaining connection to meaning.

Rate your current practices on a scale of 1–10.

(1 = never practiced, 10 = consistently practiced)

- Reflection on what matters most:
- Connection to your values in decision-making:
- Time spent on meaningful activities:
- Contribution to something larger:
- Legacy consideration:
- Meaning-making practice:

Remember: Purpose emerges through living, not through finding. You discover it by showing up authentically, contributing what you can within your current capacity, and paying attention to what creates genuine meaning in your life. Your limitations aren't obstacles to your purpose—they're often the very things that clarify it.

INTEGRATION ASSESSMENT: THE ARCHITECTURE OF MOVEMENT

Like the synovial space between our bones that enables all movement, these eight pillars work together to create possibilities in our lives. Understanding their interaction is crucial for creating sustainable movement. High-achieving professionals often experience how pressure in one area—whether it's leadership demands, relationship dynamics, or purpose alignment—creates compression across their entire system.

When a C-suite executive faces decision fatigue at work, it rarely stays contained; it affects sleep quality, personal relationships, and even financial decision-making. Similarly, creating strategic space in one dimension often triggers unexpected breakthroughs in others—like how establishing clear boundaries in your professional life can suddenly enhance your creative thinking, emotional presence with loved ones, or clarity about your long-term purpose. By mapping these interconnections in your own high-performance life, you can identify leverage points that create exponential rather than merely incremental movement.

After identifying your top three restriction points, draw connection lines between related pillars on a sheet of paper. Note how restriction in one area creates specific limitations in at least two other pillars. This visual mapping will reveal systematic patterns that a single-pillar assessment might miss.

Pillar Interaction Mapping

Identify your top three restriction points.

1. Restriction point:

    Pillar:

    Impact level (1–10):

2. Restriction point:

    Pillar:

    Impact level (1–10):

3. Restriction point:

    Pillar:

    Impact level (1–10):

Connection Analysis

- How does restriction number one affect other pillars?
- How does restriction number two affect other pillars?
- How does restriction number three affect other pillars?
- Which pillars seem most connected in your life?
- Where does creating space in one area create movement in others?

Integration Questions

- How do restrictions in one area affect movement in others?
- Where do you see patterns repeating across different dimensions?
- Which areas currently provide the most support for growth?
- How do your various life dimensions interact?
- Where might creating space in one area open movement in others?

UNDERSTANDING PILLAR CONNECTIONS: CASE STUDIES IN MOVEMENT

Key integration point: The following exercises help you move from isolated pillar understanding to system awareness. This shift from analyzing individual areas to seeing their connections represents a critical advancement in your movement journey. While individual pillar assessment is valuable, the most powerful insights often emerge when you recognize how movement in one area creates possibility in others.

Following the pattern of how the body's joint systems work together to create movement, limitations in one pillar often reveal connections to others. Consider these patterns from my early experiences.

Case Study One: Physical → Professional → Financial Connection

When my osteoarthritis first began affecting my physical movement at age seven, it didn't just limit my mobility—it created a chain of effects. My limited physical capacity affected my career options, which influenced my financial possibilities early in life. Yet understanding these connections helped me develop more comprehensive solutions rather than trying to address each challenge in isolation.

Application Exercise

Map your own pillar connection using the following framework:

1. **Identify a primary restriction.**

2. **Trace its impact on other pillars.**

   - How it affects pillar number two:
   - How it affects pillar number three:
   - How it affects pillar number four:

3. **Identify potential intervention points.**

   - Direct intervention option (action that directly addresses the primary restriction):
   - Indirect intervention option (action that addresses a connected pillar to create movement in the restricted area):
   - Systematic approach option (strategy that works with multiple pillars simultaneously to create broader change):

Case Study Two: Mental → Emotional → Purpose

Not wearing my glasses due to bullying affected more than just my vision. It influenced how I processed information, how I responded emotionally to situations, and how I navigated social spaces. This taught me that addressing any single pillar requires understanding its ripple effects through other dimensions.

Systematic Solution Mapping

When facing a complex challenge, consider the following:

1. Primary pillar affected:
2. Secondary pillars impacted:
3. Potential access points for intervention:
4. Smallest possible movement that might create systematic change:
5. How changes in one pillar might positively impact others:

UNDERSTANDING RECOVERY PATTERNS: THE REST-GROWTH CYCLE

Recovery isn't separate from movement—it's an essential component of sustainable growth. The following assessments help you recognize how your current recovery patterns either support or limit your movement potential across all pillars. Understanding these patterns is crucial for designing sustainable change rather than short-lived bursts of progress.

A degenerated joint or tendinous ossification needs recovery time when irritated. Similarly, each life dimension has its own recovery needs and patterns. Before you can recover, you need to know that there is something to recover from.

This recovery awareness addresses challenges many face in sustainable growth.

- **The sleep deficit trap:** Operating with chronically insufficient rest, creating a recovery debt that compounds over time.

- **The perpetual "on" mode:** Never allowing systems to truly reset, preventing deep restoration.

- **The numbing confusion:** Mistaking numbing behaviors for genuine recovery, and masking fatigue signals rather than addressing them.

For each dimension in the next table, identify at least two specific warning signs that indicate you need recovery and two restoration practices that have proven effective for you. Take time now to map your own recovery patterns across all eight pillars. This comprehensive assessment will reveal both your current awareness of depletion signals and the effectiveness of your restoration practices.

For each pillar, identify specific warning signs that indicate your need for recovery—these might be physical sensations, emotional states, thought patterns, or behavioral changes. Then note what this dimension requires for true restoration, what strategies you currently employ, how effective they are, and how you might improve your approach. This mapping creates the foundation for more intentional recovery practices across your entire life system.

Comprehensive Recovery Assessment
Map your recover patterns across all pillars.

Pillar	Warning Signs	Recovery Needs	Current Strategies	Effectiveness (1–10)	Improved Approach
Physical					
Mental					
Emotional					
Spiritual					
Professional					
Relational					
Financial					
Purpose					

Physical Recovery Assessment

- How long does it take to recover from different types of exertion?
- What factors speed up or slow down your physical recovery?
- How does sleep affect your recovery capacity?
- What movement patterns require more recovery time?
- What recovery practices most effectively restore your physical energy?

Mental Recovery Assessment

- How do you know when you need mental rest?
- What activities help restore your mental clarity?
- How long does it take to recover from intense focus?
- What environments support your mental recovery?
- What signs indicate you're mentally refreshed?

Emotional Recovery Assessment

- How do you process challenging emotional experiences?
- What supports your emotional resilience?
- How long do different emotional states affect you?
- What helps you return to emotional balance?
- What practices consistently restore your emotional energy?

Spiritual Recovery Assessment

- How do you reconnect with your purpose?
- What practices restore your spiritual alignment?
- What supports your spiritual resilience?
- How do you maintain spiritual boundaries?
- What activities consistently renew your sense of meaning?

Professional Recovery Assessment

- How do you recharge after intense work periods?
- What helps restore your professional motivation?
- How do you maintain work-life boundaries?
- What practices support sustainable performance?
- What warning signs indicate professional burnout?

Relational Recovery Assessment

- How do you recharge after social interactions?
- What helps restore your social energy?
- How do you maintain relationship boundaries?
- What supports healthy social engagement?
- What practices help you reconnect with yourself after extensive social activity?

Financial Recovery Assessment

- How do you rebuild after financial setbacks?
- What resources support your financial stability?
- How do you create financial buffers?
- What patterns help maintain your financial health?
- What mindset shifts support your financial recovery?

Purpose Recovery Assessment

- Reflection on what matters most:
- Connection to values in decision-making:
- Time spent on meaningful activities:
- Contribution to something larger:
- Legacy consideration:
- Meaning-making practice:

PRACTICAL IMPLEMENTATION: YOUR PERSONALIZED ASSESSMENT SYSTEM

Self-assessment is about understanding exactly where you are and where you aim to go. Just as that first rheumatologist's assessment created a foundation for understanding my physical movement potential, this evaluation across all eight pillars will provide the basis for your next movements.

Action prioritization framework: After completing all assessments, identify the following:

1. Your most restricted pillar (lowest scores)
2. The pillar with the greatest movement potential (highest engagement but with clear restrictions)
3. The pillar with the strongest connections to other areas

These three areas often provide the most effective starting points for creating movement in your entire system. While you may be drawn to focus on areas of greatest interest, beginning with these strategic points typically creates more significant and sustainable change.

Now that you understand the importance of regular assessment across all pillars, it's time to create your personalized implementation plan. The following framework transforms assessment from a one-time event into an ongoing practice that guides your movement journey. This structured approach ensures you'll not only gather valuable insights but actually apply them to create meaningful change. Take time to customize each element of this plan to your specific circumstances and schedule, making it a sustainable part of your routine rather than an overwhelming addition to your to-do list.

Ninety-Day Assessment Implementation Plan

A. **Starting Assessment**

- Complete the full eight pillars assessment within the next seven days.
- Identify your top three restriction points and their interconnections.
- Map your recovery patterns across all dimensions.

B. **Weekly Check-in Protocol**

- Day of week:
- Time:
- Areas to assess:
- Documentation method:
- Key questions to ask:

C. **Monthly Deep-Dive Schedule**

- Date:
- Focus areas:
- Review method:
- Adjustment protocol:

D. **Ninety-Day Reassessment Plan**

- Date:
- Comprehensive review process:
- Progress measurement approach:
- Next phase planning method:

ASSESSMENT TOOLS FOR IMMEDIATE IMPLEMENTATION

Daily Movement Check-In

Below is a three-minute template to track your daily movement capacity.

Date:

Time:

Physical energy (1–10):

Mental clarity (1–10):

Emotional balance (1–10):

Purpose connection (1–10):

Today's restriction point:

Today's movement potential:

One small action to create space:

Weekly Movement Review

Dedicate fifty to thirty minutes each week to this deeper check-in.

Week of:

Pillar Review

- Most restricted pillar this week:
- Most fluid pillar this week:
- Most significant change observed:

Pattern Recognition

- Recurring restriction:
- Emerging potential:
- Unexpected connection:

Recovery Analysis

- Recovery needs identified:
- Effective recovery practices:
- Recovery adjustments needed:

Next Week's Focus

- Priority pillar:
- Specific space to create:
- Support needed:

CHAPTER INTEGRATION: PUTTING IT ALL TOGETHER

Understanding your current architecture is the essential first step in creating meaningful movement. In this chapter, we've explored the following:

- The importance of comprehensive assessment across all life dimensions
- How to identify restriction points and their interconnections
- The necessity of understanding recovery patterns
- Tools for creating sustainable assessment practices

Remember: Assessment is not about judgment, but about creating precise awareness that enables intentional movement. Now that your anchor is firmly cast and positioned, we can slowly up-anchor and cast sail toward understanding how architecture enables smart movement choices in all areas of life.

The comprehensive assessment you've just completed serves as your movement blueprint—a detailed map showing both your current restrictions and your potential pathways forward. Rather than seeing this assessment as a one-time exercise, consider it the foundation of an ongoing awareness practice. By regularly checking in with each pillar and its connections, you'll develop increasing sensitivity to subtle shifts and emerging possibilities.

The insights from this assessment don't just inform you—they prepare you for the narrative revision work in the next chapter. Understanding where you are is the essential first step in rewriting the stories that have defined your movement patterns.

Key Chapter Takeaways

1. Comprehensive assessment must precede effective action.
2. The eight pillars are interconnected, creating a unified system.
3. Recovery patterns are essential to sustainable growth.
4. Regular assessment creates the foundation for meaningful change.
5. Small, consistent check-ins create better awareness than occasional deep dives.

Your Immediate Next Steps

1. Complete the full Eight Pillars Assessment.
2. Identify your top three restriction points.
3. Map the connections between these restrictions and other pillars.
4. Develop your personalized assessment schedule.
5. Implement your first daily and weekly check-in protocols.

Commitment moment: When specifically will you complete your initial Eight Pillars Assessment?

Date:

Time:

Support needed:

Potential obstacles:

Strategy to overcome obstacles:

Reward for completion:

In the next chapter, we'll explore how to rewrite the narratives that have defined your movement patterns. Using the assessment insights you've gained, you'll learn to create new stories that enable rather than restrict your potential.

THREE

REWRITING PERSONAL NARRATIVES

CREATING SPACE FOR NEW STORIES

Who This Chapter Is For

- Individuals struggling with limiting self-narratives
- Professionals seeking to overcome performance barriers
- Leaders ready to transform their personal stories
- Anyone whose past narratives are restricting their future potential

Key Transformational Outcomes

By the end of this chapter, you will be able to do the following:

- Understand how personal narratives shape your movement potential
- Identify restrictive stories that limit your growth
- Develop a framework for narrative transformation
- Create practical strategies for story revision across all eight pillars
- Build a sustainable system for ongoing narrative evolution

THE POWER OF PERSONAL NARRATIVES

Just as our bodies create protective movement patterns in response to pain, our minds develop protective narratives in response to trauma. These stories become the invisible architecture that shapes how we move through life. Like the synovial space between our joints, the space between what happened to us and how we carry it determines our freedom of movement.

This chapter guides you through a systematic process of narrative revision—identifying the stories that limit your movement, understanding their origins, and creating new narratives that enable rather than restrict your growth. We'll explore this transformation across all eight pillars, providing practical tools for rewriting the stories that have defined your movement patterns until now.

Reflection Point

What stories do you tell yourself about who you are and what's possible?

How have these narratives shaped your movement in the world?

Which stories feel most restrictive to your growth?

My Narrative Transformation Journey

Beginning my personal transformation with therapists, coaches, and mentors in my midtwenties taught me this fundamental truth: Through their guidance, I began healing from negative personal narratives that had formed in my subconscious, creating measurable steps toward my goals. Life was gaining meaningful traction—until September 11, 2001, when the narratives I had carefully constructed about safety, purpose, and possibility were shattered in a single morning.

But to understand how that day rewrote my story, you first need to know how I had learned to read the stories written in space.

Key insight: Our most profound transformations often come when our existing narratives are disrupted, creating space for new stories to emerge.

THE LANGUAGE OF LIMITATION: UNDERSTANDING NARRATIVE RESTRICTION

Growing up with osteoarthritis, I became fluent in the language of restricted movement. Each morning, my joints would tell their story of limitation, and each day, I had to decide how to respond to that story. Would I let pain write my narrative of what was possible, or could I find new ways to move within the space I had? This daily dialogue with my physical limitations became my first lesson in narrative revision.

This process of narrative revision addresses challenges many face with their own internal stories.

- **The victim trap:** Remaining trapped in narratives where external circumstances control everything.
- **The inherited script:** Operating from stories about what success "should" look like.
- **The impostor narrative:** Believing accomplishments are fraudulent and success is temporary.

These internal stories often create more restriction than any external circumstance, compressing the space where authentic movement could otherwise flourish.

Core assessment exercise: This narrative mapping is foundational to the work in this chapter. Take time to identify your dominant stories in each category, noting their impact on your movement. The more honest you can be about limiting narratives, the more powerful your revision process will become. Complete this exercise before moving to pillar-specific work. Take time with this exercise, as it forms the foundation for your narrative revision work. Consider writing two or three sentences for each story rather than giving a single-word response.

Narrative Assessment Framework
Identify your dominant life narratives using this mapping exercise.

Narrative Category	Your Current Story	Origin	Impact on Movement (1– 10)	Potential Revision
Identity ("I am …")				
Capability ("I can/can't …")				
Deserving ("I deserve/don't deserve…")				
Purpose ("My purpose is …")				
Possibility ("What's possible is …")				
Relationships ("Others are …")				
World ("The world is …")				
Future ("My future will …")				

Activism and Narrative Evolution

By 1998, my youthful journey with chronic pain, combined with my lived experiences in Brooklyn, led me to Cures Not Wars, a nonprofit organization in New York City. My role in helping establish the first global Million Marijuana March created a profound sense of empowerment while I found effective pain management freed mental space that had been previously consumed by constant pain signals. Yet this experience taught me something crucial about balance: Solutions often carry unintended consequences.

What began as advocacy for medical access evolved in ways I hadn't anticipated, with recreational use potentially creating stagnation rather than movement for some. This evolution perfectly illustrates the core principle of the Synovial Space methodology: Sustainable growth isn't about maximizing freedom in one area but about finding the optimal balance point across all dimensions of life. Like the perfect amount of synovial fluid in a joint, the right balance creates movement, while too much or too little leads to restriction.

Coaching Moment: Understanding Your Stories

Take a moment to reflect on your own narrative foundations:

- What stories form the architecture of your daily movements?
- Which narratives feel protective?
- Which feel restrictive?
- Where might you be ready for revision?

Document your answers in this framework.

Narrative Type	Current Story	Serves Me By ...	Restricts Me By ...	Ready for Revision?
Physical Capacity				
Mental Clarity				
Emotional Range				
Spiritual Connection				
Professional Potential				
Relational Range				
Financial Possibility				
Purpose Alignment				

Understanding the language of limitation is the first step in narrative transformation. Now let's explore how significant life events can create dramatic turning points in our personal stories—moments that both challenge our existing narratives and create space for new ones to emerge.

WHEN STORIES SHATTER: THE 9/11 EXPERIENCE

After years of navigating both physical and emotional pain alongside career uncertainties, my life had begun to find a rhythm of stability. Then came that crystalline September morning. I had just settled into my new fifth-floor walk-up in Spanish Harlem and was adjusting to life as an administrative assistant at a insurance company called Guardian Life. My commute to 7 Hanover Square had become a morning ritual of possibility—walking to the train, navigating the streets of Spanish Harlem, and emerging into the pulsing heart of Wall Street. Each day, I used this transition time to write my own story of success, sketching poems, business plans, and morning pages on the subway.

The sky was a perfect blue canvas that morning, the kind that makes you believe anything is possible. I had no way of knowing that within hours, that same sky would become the backdrop for a narrative that would change not just my story but the story of an entire city.

Narrative Assessment: Foundations of Safety and Certainty

Take inventory of your current life stories.

Safety Stories Assessment

- What makes you feel secure?
- How do you respond when security is threatened?
- What protection patterns have you developed?
- What narratives about safety guide your decisions?

Movement Stories Assessment

- Where do you move freely in life?
- Where do you feel restricted?
- What patterns guide your daily navigation?
- What stories determine where you will or won't go?

Purpose Stories Assessment

- What gives your life meaning?
- How do you respond when your purpose feels threatened?
- What new stories might be waiting to emerge?
- How does your purpose narrative shape your choices?

THE SPACE BETWEEN STORIES: NAVIGATING LIFE'S TRANSITIONS

As I settled at my desk that morning, the first signs appeared in my peripheral vision: wads of paper floated past my window on the east side of the building. I thought there had been a ticker-tape parade. I didn't know a plane had hit the North Tower. I must have been in the elevator at the time. Then came the distinctive roar, impact, and whoosh of the second plane that shattered not just glass and steel but every story I had written about safety and certainty.

I found myself running up Second Avenue that morning after walking past my old high school, Murry Bergtraum. I had overheard teens celebrating the school closure due to the attack. The jeers struck a nerve, and I started running to get away from their youthful ignorance.

As I ran up Second Avenue, my body creating rapid movement despite my osteoarthritis, I experienced firsthand how quickly our narratives can shift. With each block, I passed landmarks that had once represented success and stability: the Empire State Building, the Chrysler Building, the United Nations. Now these same structures loomed as potential targets, their familiar silhouettes transformed by a new narrative of vulnerability.

Integration Practice: Mapping Your Narrative Shifts

Consider a time when your stories suddenly changed.

    A. **The event that triggered the shift:**

    B. **What were your narratives before the event?**

- About yourself:
- About others:
- About the world:

    C. **What were your narratives after the event?**

- About yourself:
- About others:
- About the world:

    D. **What familiar landmarks became threatening?**
    E. **How did your movement patterns adapt?**
    F. **Where did you find new space for possibility?**

Application guidance: This framework helps you navigate major transitions by identifying where you are in the narrative shift process. For each stage, document your current experience, challenges you're facing, emerging opportunities, and the specific support you need. This creates a road map through territory that often feels disorienting without clear markers.

Narrative Transition Framework
When experiencing a major narrative disruption:

Stage	Experience	Challenges	Opportunities	Support Needed
Disorientation				
Destabilization				
Grief/Loss				
Meaning-Making				
Integration				
New Story				

Major transitions create the potential for narrative revision, but this potential isn't automatically realized. The next step is consciously engaging in the art of creating new stories that enable rather than restrict movement.

FINDING MOVEMENT IN NEW STORIES: THE ART OF NARRATIVE REVISION

In the days that followed, I discovered something crucial about narrative transformation: Just as our synovial spaces need the right amount of fluid for optimal movement, our life stories need the right amount of space between experience and interpretation. Too little space, and we become trapped in rigid narratives. Too much space, and we lose our sense of coherence and direction.

I saw this playing out in the following ways:

- Some colleagues remained frozen in their old stories, unable to adapt
- Others completely abandoned their previous narratives, losing their anchors
- A few found ways to create new stories that honored both the past and the future

Coaching Moment: Story Flexibility Assessment

Just as manual therapists can assess joint mobility, let's examine your narrative flexibility.

- Where do you tend to freeze in old stories?
- Where might you be too quick to abandon previous narratives?
- How do you balance honoring the past while creating space for new possibilities?

Rate your narrative flexibility in each dimension (1–10).

(1 = completely rigid, 10 = optimally flexible)

- Physical story flexibility:
- Mental story flexibility:
- Emotional story flexibility:
- Spiritual story flexibility:
- Professional story flexibility:
- Relational story flexibility:
- Financial story flexibility:
- Purpose story flexibility:

THE EIGHT PILLARS OF NARRATIVE REVISION

This is where the Eight Pillars framework becomes crucial. Each pillar represents a dimension of your life story you can examine for potential revision before, during, and after significant change. Like a manual therapist helping patients rebuild movement patterns after an injury, this framework helps you reconstruct your narratives in ways that enable rather than restrict growth.

Implementation approach: The following sections provide specific tools for revising narratives in each pillar. While you may be drawn to begin with pillars that are most relevant to your current challenges, I recommend working through all eight areas to uncover less obvious narrative restrictions. For each pillar, first identify limiting stories, then explore their origins, and finally, develop alternative narratives that create more movement potential.

Our exploration of narrative revision begins where movement is most tangible: in our physical stories. The tales we tell about our bodies create the foundation for all other dimensions of movement.

1. Physical Narrative Revision

The first stories we need to examine are often the most literal—the ones written in our physical movement. Through my life journey with osteoarthritis, I learned that the stories we tell about our physical limitations often become self-fulfilling prophecies. At first, my narrative was simple: Feeling pain meant I had to stop whatever I was doing. But gradually, I learned to rewrite this story from "I can't move because of pain" to "How can I create movement within these parameters?"

Walking through Manhattan in the weeks after 9/11, I witnessed a city transformed by collective trauma. The somber mood was palpable everywhere—in cautious gazes, in the deliberate distance people kept from landmarks, in the new rituals of vigilance that had emerged. My own routes changed, as did those of countless others navigating this altered landscape. These weren't just physical adjustments—they were new stories being written in space and movement, visible evidence of how narratives reshape our physical relationships with the world.

Now it's time to examine your own physical narratives—the stories that shape how you move through the world. The table below helps you identify limiting beliefs about your body and transform them into narratives that create more possibility. For each statement pattern, identify a specific belief you hold about your physical capacity, note where this story originated, and honestly assess how it impacts your movement. Then create an alternative narrative that acknowledges reality while opening more possibilities, and identify one small step you can take to begin embodying this new story. Remember that changing deep-seated physical narratives happens gradually through consistent practice rather than overnight transformation.

Physical Narrative Revision Tool Kit
Map your physical movement stories.

Current Physical Narrative	Origin	Impact on Movement	Alternative Narrative	Small Step to Shift
"I can't …"				
"My body always …"				
"Because of my condition …"				
"I'll never be able to …"				

Physical Adaptation Assessment

- What compensations have you developed?
- Which adaptations serve you, and which limit you?
- Where might new movement patterns be possible?

Action Plan for Physical Narrative Revision

A. **Daily Awareness Practice**

- Notice moments when you automatically interpret pain as a signal to stop completely.
- Identify which movement limitations are truly physical and which are maintained by habit.
- Record recurring thoughts or beliefs that emerge during physical activities.

B. **Narrative Shift Protocol**

- Select one limiting physical story you're ready to rewrite.
- Develop a new narrative focused on possibilities within your current capacity.
- Determine a minimal physical action that represents this new perspective.
- Consistently practice both the new thought pattern and movement for twenty-one days.

C. **Progress Documentation**

- Describe physical sensations you experience while embodying your revised narrative.
- Monitor gradual increases in your movement range and capacity.
- Note how your emotional state shifts as your physical narrative evolves.
- While physical stories often have the most immediate impact on your movement, mental narratives shape how you interpret and respond to every experience. Let's explore how revising these thought patterns creates new space for growth.

2. Mental Narrative Revision

After 9/11, I found myself at the Metropolitan Museum of Art, a sanctuary I had discovered years earlier during my darkest high school days. But this time was different. Where once I had used art to escape reality, now I needed it to make sense of a reality that defied comprehension.

This shift mirrors what happens in our synovial spaces during rehabilitation. Just as a joint must learn new movement patterns after an injury, our minds must learn new ways of creating meaning after trauma. The key isn't to erase the old patterns but to build new ones that serve our current needs.

Mental Narrative Revision Framework
Identify your mental movement patterns.

Mental Pattern	Trigger Situations	Impact on Choices	Alternative Perspective	Implementation Strategy
Black-and-White Thinking				
Catastrophizing				
Mind Reading				
"Should" Statements				
Labeling				

Pattern Assessment

- Which thought patterns still serve you?
- Which ones have become restrictive?
- What new mental movements feel possible?

Mental Narrative Revision Protocol

A. **Thought Tracking Practice**

- For one week, record specific repetitive thoughts that arise throughout your day.
- Identify specific circumstances or people that consistently trigger limiting beliefs.
- Document how these thought patterns affect your actions and decisions.

B. **Narrative Transformation Exercise**

- Choose one recurring thought pattern that consistently limits your potential.
- Write out three different ways to interpret the same situation or challenge.
- Spend one full day operating from each new perspective, noting the results.
- Adopt the viewpoint that creates the most positive change in your behavior.

C. **Mental Flexibility Development**

- Schedule brief daily practices where you deliberately view situations from multiple angles.
- Establish specific phrases or physical gestures that interrupt your habitual thought patterns.
- Implement a five-minute daily practice that strengthens your mental adaptability.
- Your thoughts and emotions are intimately connected, with each influencing the other. Emotional narratives determine not just how you feel but what feelings you allow yourself to express authentically.

3. Emotional Narrative Revision

Before 9/11, I found emotional release through spoken-word poetry at the Nuyorican Poets Cafe in the Lower East Side. Poetry had become one of my synovial spaces where I could move freely despite my life's restrictions. Every Wednesday and Friday night, I would transform pain into performance, using rhythm and wordplay to create movement where trauma had tried to create rigidity.

But something shifted after that September morning. Standing before a crowd, sharing a piece about Casey Cho—my friend who never made it out of the North Tower—I realized I wasn't creating new emotional movement. Like a joint that develops compensatory patterns, I had created sophisticated ways of performing emotion rather than processing it.

This realization hit me like moments in physical therapy when I discovered I'd been strengthening the wrong muscles. Poetry had served its purpose—it had been the synovial fluid that kept me moving when everything else felt frozen. But now it was time to find new space, new movement, and new patterns.

Take a moment now to examine your own patterns of emotional expression using the framework below. For each core emotion, reflect on how you typically express (or suppress) it in your daily life. Then honestly assess to what degree this expression is authentic or performative on a scale of one to ten, with ten being completely authentic. Consider what alternative expressions might feel more genuine, even if they're less familiar or comfortable. Finally, identify what support you might need —whether from others, environments, or personal practices—to move toward more authentic emotional expression. This assessment isn't about judging your current patterns but about creating space for more genuine emotional movement.

Emotional Narrative Transformation Tool Kit
Emotional Movement Assessment

Emotion	How I Typically Express It	Authentic vs. Performative (1–10)	Alternative Expression	Support Needed
Anger				
Fear				
Grief				
Joy				
Shame				

Performance versus Processing Assessment

- Where do you perform emotions rather than feel them?
- What emotions do you tend to repeat or get stuck in?
- How might you be using emotional expression as a shield?

Action Plan for Emotional Revision

Emotion Authenticity Practice

- Document moments when you're displaying emotions for others versus actually feeling them.
- Identify which specific emotions you tend to exaggerate or perform for effect.
- List environments and relationships where you feel safe enough to express genuine feelings.

D. **Emotional Vocabulary Expansion**

- Build a personal list of at least thirty specific emotion words beyond basic happy / sad / angry terms.
- Practice identifying and naming subtle emotional variations during daily check-ins.
- Connect bodily sensations (tightness, warmth, tension) to specific emotional states.

E. **Integration Protocol**

- Write about your actual feelings, without editing or performing them for an imagined audience.
- Begin expressing authentic emotions with one trusted person before expanding your circle.
- Record instances when genuine emotional expression deepened a connection or resolved an issue.

Authentic Expression Framework

When experiencing strong emotions, use this progression:

1. Name: "I am feeling _____."
2. Locate: "I feel it in my _____."
3. Scale: "The intensity is ___ out of 10."
4. Need: "What I need right now is _____."
5. Action: "A small step I can take is _____."

As you reshape your emotional stories, you naturally encounter questions of meaning and purpose. Spiritual narratives provide the context that gives significance to all your other stories.

4. Spiritual Narrative Revision

The collapse of the towers created a void in the Manhattan skyline—a visible reminder of how quickly certainty can transform into empty space. But just as our joints teach us that space isn't empty—that synovial fluid fills the gaps between bones with possibility—I learned that spiritual voids can become spaces for new meaning to emerge.

Growing up, I had pinned my sense of purpose on joining the military's special operations, only to be disqualified by color vision deficiency and other predispositions. Having to quit the delayed entry program created a similar void—an empty space where certainty and purpose had once lived. Rather than face my limitations and loss of identity, I searched desperately for something, anything, that could provide the same clear sense of direction and meaning. Like many before me, I discovered that our most beautiful attempts at meaning-making can become their own kind of cage.

Now let's examine your own spiritual landscape using the framework below. This assessment helps you recognize which spiritual beliefs truly resonate with your authentic self and which beliefs you may have inherited or outgrown. For each category, identify a key belief that has shaped how you understand that aspect of life, then note its origin—whether from family, culture, personal experience, or formal teaching. Honestly assess how deeply it still resonates with you and how effectively it serves your growth. Finally, consider how this belief might evolve to better support your authentic movement. Approach this exercise with curiosity rather than judgment, recognizing that spiritual evolution is a natural part of the human journey.

Spiritual Narrative Revision Tool Kit
Pattern Recognition Exercise: Spiritual Space Mapping

Spiritual Belief	Origin	Still Resonant? (1–10)	Serves Growth? (1–10)	Potential Evolution
About purpose				
About suffering				
About connection				
About meaning				
About death				

Meaning Assessment

- Which practices truly nurture your growth?
- Where might intense dedication be masking avoidance?
- How do your beliefs about success and failure create or restrict your movement?

Action Plan for Spiritual Revision

A. **Practice Assessment**

- Identify when you're engaging in spiritual activities out of obligation rather than genuine connection.
- Record specific moments when you felt authentically connected to something larger than yourself.
- Recognize where your need for "doing it right" prevents a deeper spiritual experience.

B. **Meaning-Making Framework**

- Start a dedicated journal for important questions, giving them time to unfold without forcing answers.
- Schedule regular periods of silent reflection without seeking immediate insights or conclusions.
- Practice holding contradictory ideas simultaneously, rather than needing to resolve them.

C. **Integration Steps**

- Remove one obligation-based spiritual practice that no longer serves your authentic growth.
- Try one new form of spiritual expression each week for a month, noting which resonate most deeply.
- Create a flexible spiritual practice that balances consistent structure with room for spontaneity.
- Your spiritual understanding influences how you express yourself in the world, particularly through your work. Professional narratives shape not just what you do but how you create value and meaning through your contributions.

5. Professional Narrative Revision

My time spent as an administrative assistant at Guardian Life Insurance showed me something profound about my professional identity. Before 9/11, success meant performing well within established structures. But watching colleagues break down over lost family members at the World Trade Center, while others remained frozen at their desks, revealed how quickly professional protocols can become meaningless in the face of human tragedy.

The decision to run home that day wasn't in any employee handbook. Neither was reflecting on the next steps in my bathtub, while still dressed in my business suit. These moments forced me to rewrite my understanding of professional life from "following established protocols" to "responding to human needs in the moment."

Take time now to examine your own professional narratives using the framework below. These stories about work, success, and professional identity often operate below conscious awareness yet powerfully shape your career choices and satisfaction. For each narrative category, identify the story you currently tell yourself, assess its impact on your professional life, and honestly evaluate how well it serves your growth. Then develop an alternative narrative that better aligns with your authentic values, and identify specific strategies for implementing this new perspective. Remember that transforming deep-seated professional stories happens gradually through consistent practice in real workplace situations.

Professional Narrative Transformation Framework
Pattern Recognition Exercise: Professional Space Mapping

Professional Narrative	Current Impact	Serves Growth? (1–10)	Alternative Story	Implementation Strategy
"Success means …"				
"My value comes from …"				
"My career should …"				
"Professionals must …"				

Response Assessment

- How do you handle professional disruption?
- When do protocols help, and when do they hinder?
- What unexpected strengths emerge in crisis?

Action Plan for Professional Revision

A. **Pattern Identification**

- Record situations where you respond with automatic professional habits rather than conscious choices.
- Identify specific instances when following procedures created barriers to meeting people's needs.
- Document moments when you had to adapt standard protocols to address unique circumstances.

B. **Value Clarification**

- List five aspects of your work that bring genuine satisfaction beyond salary or status.
- Compare your organization's success metrics with what personally gives you a sense of accomplishment.
- Develop three specific criteria for professional fulfillment that align with your personal values.

C. **Integration Steps**

- Select one self-imposed professional "rule" to let go of that doesn't actually serve your effectiveness.
- Create boundaries that protect creative thinking time alongside structured periods of productivity.
- Implement a decision-making framework that balances procedural requirements with human considerations.
- Identify three ways to bring more of your authentic strengths into your current professional role.

Your professional narratives about contribution and value naturally connect to how you view resources in your life. Financial narratives reveal deep beliefs about worth, sufficiency, and possibility that often originate in your earliest experiences with abundance and scarcity.

6. Relational Narrative Revision

The relationships that sustained me before 9/11 took on new meaning in its aftermath. Some friends couldn't comprehend the psychological impact of being present during the attacks, while others who hadn't been there seemed to understand instinctively. These unexpected connections and disconnections taught me that our relational narratives—who we trust, how we connect, and what we expect from others—can shift dramatically when our personal stories change.

Now let's explore the stories that shape your connections with others. The framework below helps you identify the underlying beliefs that influence how you approach relationships, where these narratives originated, and how they affect your capacity for authentic connection. For each relational belief, assess its impact on your interactions and how well it serves your growth. Then develop an alternative narrative that creates more space for genuine connection while still honoring your needs and boundaries. This revision process isn't about creating "perfect" relationships but about freeing yourself from limiting stories that restrict meaningful connections with others.

Relational Narrative Transformation Tool Kit
Pattern Recognition Exercise: Relationship Story Mapping

Relationship Belief	Origin	Impact on Connections	Serves Growth? (1–10)	Alternative Narrative
"Trust means …"				
"Others will …"				
"I must …"				
"Connection requires …"				
"Relationships should …"				

Connection Assessment

- How do your relationship stories affect your connections?
- Where do you create unnecessary barriers?
- What expectations limit your ability to authentically relate to others?

Action Plan for Relational Revision

A. Pattern Identification

- Record repeating interaction patterns in your key relationships (e.g., caretaking, withdrawing, controlling).
- Identify when specific current relationship reactions stem from past experiences with different people.
- Note how your internal stories about relationships affect your openness and communication style.

B. Story Transformation

- Select one specific belief about relationships that consistently limits connection (e.g., "people always leave").
- Write a new, more balanced narrative that acknowledges past experiences while allowing for new possibilities.
- Practice this new perspective in lower-stakes interactions before applying it to crucial relationships.

C. **Integration Strategy**

- Each day, implement one new relationship behavior that aligns with your revised narrative.
- Share your growth goals with a trusted friend who can provide feedback on your progress.
- Create a list of specific situations that typically activate old relationship patterns.
- Schedule regular opportunities for authentic sharing that gradually increase in vulnerability.

7. Financial Narrative Revision

Working in the Financial District during 9/11 exposed a stark truth about financial security. One moment, I was part of the seemingly invincible Wall Street machine; the next, I was watching paper flutter past my window, and everything felt fragile and temporary. The financial center of the world had become a war zone, and with it, my sense of occupational security at the time crumbled.

I was too young and poor when the Gulf War recession hit to fully appreciate the impact of a downward economic period. When the events of 9/11 nudged the dot-com bubble further into a recessionary period, this jarring shift challenged my assumptions about stability in the financial sector. But just as our synovial spaces need both flexibility and structure, I learned that true financial resilience comes not from rigid institutional strength but from our ability to adapt and create new movement patterns.

Take time now to examine your own financial narratives using the framework below. The stories we tell ourselves about money and resources often operate beneath conscious awareness yet powerfully shape our financial decisions and possibilities. For each belief category, identify the specific story you currently tell yourself, note its origin, assess how it impacts your decisions, and evaluate whether it truly serves your growth. Then develop an alternative perspective that better aligns with your authentic values, and identify concrete strategies for implementing this new financial mindset. Remember that transforming deep-seated financial stories happens gradually through consistent practice in real-world situations rather than through sudden insight alone. We are not manifesting new realities out of thin air here. We are uncovering your financial narratives. Uncovering your narratives is the first step toward progressive growth.

Financial Narrative Transformation Tool Kit

Pattern Recognition Exercise: Financial Space Mapping

Financial Belief	Origin	Impact on Decisions	Serves Growth? (1–10)	Alternative Perspective
"Money is …"				
"Financial security means …"				
"My financial worth is …"				
"I deserve …"				
"Financial success requires …"				

Security Assessment

- What defines financial stability for you?
- How do external events shape your sense of security?
- Where might you need to build more resilience?

Action Plan for Financial Revision

A. Pattern Recognition

- Track your emotional and behavioral responses when facing financial uncertainty.
- Identify situations where you rely on institutional authority rather than on your personal judgments about money.
- List areas where creating more financial flexibility would reduce anxiety and increase your options.

B. Belief Transformation

- Write down money messages you received from family members while growing up.
- Question assumptions about wealth, saving, or spending that you've never personally verified.
- Develop three new empowering beliefs about money that align with your current values and goals.

C. **Adaptability Development**

- Create a plan for generating income from at least three different sources.
- Develop skills that maintain their value across different economic environments.
- Establish an emergency fund and alternative resource networks for unexpected challenges.
- Schedule monthly reviews to assess how your financial narratives are evolving.

Just as your financial stories shape your relationship with resources, your environmental narratives determine how you interact with the spaces you inhabit. The stories you tell about your physical environments—both built and natural—profoundly affect your movement patterns and sense of possibility.

8. Purpose Narrative Revision

Purpose narratives differ from other pillar narratives in a fundamental way—they integrate everything else. Your story about your purpose draws from your physical experiences, your mental frameworks, your emotional capacity, your spiritual understanding, your professional expression, your relational connections, and your financial reality. These aren't separate narratives competing for dominance—they're threads weaving together into the larger story of why you're here and what you're here to contribute.

Before chronic pain forced me to directly confront my purpose narrative, I carried an unconscious story. That story was that purpose meant making a grand impact. In high school, my vision was clear: I would join The US Marine Corps through their delayed entry program, earn my way into special operations, and become part of an elite force—a band of brothers and sisters united in something greater than ourselves. When I learned that I couldn't pursue that path—that my color vision deficiency closed me off from not only special operations and law enforcement but numerous other fields I'd been drawn to—it shattered more than my career plan. My sense of purpose had been eliminated before I'd ever started. This created years of drastic doubt. If I couldn't serve in those ways, was I living purposefully at all?

Then physical limitations made "grand" impossible. The restriction forced examination: What if purpose isn't about scale? What if it's about alignment? What if showing up faithfully with the capacity I have—creating meaning in small ways and contributing what I can within my limitations —isn't settling for less but discovering what matters most?

That narrative revision changed everything. Not because it lowered my standards but because it revealed what I'd been missing: Purpose isn't performed for others' recognition. It's lived for your own soul's alignment. Purpose doesn't require a platform. It happens in how you show up when no one's watching, in the choices you make that only you know about, and in the integrity you maintain when it costs you something.

As I examined my own purpose narrative, I began recognizing similar patterns in others. The stories we tell ourselves about meaning and contribution often share common themes—narratives that either expand or restrict how we understand our lives' significance. These narratives are rarely conscious. We inherit them from our cultures, absorb them from achievement-focused environments, or construct them as protection against feeling insignificant. But when left unexamined, they shape everything: what we attempt, what we avoid, and what we consider "enough."

Common Purpose Narratives

The following narratives shape how you approach meaning, contribution, and direction:

- "I haven't found my purpose yet": Treats purpose as a hidden treasure requiring discovery rather than as meaning created through living.
- "My purpose should be bigger than this": Creates constant inadequacy by measuring significance through an external scale rather than through internal alignment
- "Purpose means sacrificing everything else": Assumes that meaning requires abandoning other life dimensions rather than integrating them
- "I'm too old/young to have purpose": Restricts contribution by age rather than recognizing that purpose evolves throughout our lives
- "Real purpose requires a grand impact": Dismisses quiet significance in favor of visible achievement
- "My life is too ordinary to have purpose": Confuses dramatic circumstances with meaningful living
- "Focusing on purpose is selfish when others need practical help": Creates a false dichotomy between meaning and responsibility

Recognizing these narratives is the first step. But recognition alone doesn't change them. These stories have deep roots—some planted in childhood, others reinforced through years of repetition. They feel like truth rather than interpretation. The work isn't to force yourself to believe something different, but to examine what you currently believe and ask whether it serves you. Whether it's accurate. Whether it creates the life you want or restricts it.

The framework below guides this examination. It's not quick. Purpose narratives don't shift through intellectual understanding alone—they change through consistent, honest reflection and deliberate practice. But they do change. I know because mine did.

Purpose Narrative Transformation Tool Kit

Use this framework to identify and revise your purpose narratives.

Step One: Identify Your Current Purpose Story

- Complete this sentence: "My purpose in life is limited by …"
- What do you believe about finding versus creating purpose?
- How do you measure whether your life has meaning?
- What would need to be true for you to feel purposeful?

Step Two: Trace the Narrative Origin

- Where did you learn your beliefs about purpose?
- Which cultural messages shaped your understanding of meaningful living?
- What family patterns influenced your sense of calling?
- How have past experiences reinforced or challenged these narratives?

Step Three: Examine the Cost

- How does this narrative restrict your capacity for meaningful living?
- What possibilities does it close?
- How does it affect your other pillars?
- What would become possible if this narrative shifted?

Pattern Recognition Exercise: Purpose Space Mapping

This exercise helps you identify where your purpose narrative manifests in your daily life.

Track your sense of meaning for one week. Each evening, rate your sense of purpose that day (1–10) and note the following:

- Activities that created genuine meaning:
- Moments when you felt aligned with your values:
- Times when you dismissed small significance:
- Situations where you waited for "real" purpose:
- Instances where you contributed without receiving recognition:

At the week's end, review your tracking. What patterns reveal your current purpose narrative? Where does it serve you? Where does it restrict you?

This awareness creates choice. You can't revise what you can't see, but once you see it clearly, the narrative loses some of its unconscious power. You begin recognizing the story as interpretation rather than fact. That recognition opens space for something different.

Awareness alone isn't enough, however. The old narrative won't simply disappear because you've identified it. It's been reinforced through years of repetition, validated by results (even painful ones), and woven into your identity. Revision requires intention. Not forced optimism or manufactured belief, but the deliberate construction of an alternative story—one you test against reality, refine through experience, and choose repeatedly and progressively until it becomes as automatic as the narrative it's replacing.

Action Plan for Purpose Narrative Revision

Create your revision strategy.

Your current purpose narrative:

- Evidence supporting your alternative narrative:
    - List experiences where meaning emerged without being on a grand scale, where contribution mattered despite lack of recognition, and where purpose revealed itself through living rather than searching.

- Your revised purpose narrative:
- Daily practice:
    - How will you practice this new narrative? (Morning reflection on what matters most? Evening documentation of meaning created? Weekly review of values alignment?)

Remember: Purpose isn't found—it's revealed through authentic living. Your work isn't to discover some hidden calling but to show up fully with the capacity you have, contribute what you can, and pay attention to what creates genuine meaning. Your limitations aren't obstacles to purpose. They're often exactly what clarifies it.

INTEGRATION: TRANSFORMING RESTRICTION INTO PURPOSE

The narrative revision work you've done across all eight pillars now converges into a unified approach to transformation. This integration phase is where individual story changes combine to create a coherent new narrative about who you are and what's possible in your life.

Understanding how to rewrite our stories opens new possibilities for movement. But just as physical movement requires both flexibility and strength, our new narratives need both space and structure.

After leaving the poetry scene, I faced the same question many of us confront when we leave our familiar patterns: Now what?

My first attempt at transformation—taking an executive administrative assistant role at the Food Bank for New York City—taught me something crucial about timing: Sometimes, our stories need more rewriting before we can fully embody new patterns. Like trying to run before relearning how to walk, I had attempted to help others in a new role before fully vetting the circumstances. It was the wrong landing pad for my life story, but I was so desperate to remove myself from Lower Manhattan that I did not heed the warning signs of a misaligned opportunity. This was the first role I was relieved from against my will.

But here's what I've learned about failure in movement: It's information, not destination. Being terminated from my role at the Food Bank for New York City opened up a new pathway: massage therapy and personal training school. Here was a way to directly translate my understanding of restriction into liberation—not just for myself but for others.

The narrative revision work you've done across all eight pillars now needs to be translated into practical action. The following implementation plan helps you systematically transform insights into daily practices and conscious choices. Rather than attempting to revise all your stories simultaneously, this structured approach guides you to select one narrative to begin with, focusing on consistency and integration rather than on speed. By following this thirty-day protocol, you'll create the foundation for sustainable narrative transformation that gradually extends to all dimensions of your life.

NARRATIVE TRANSFORMATION IMPLEMENTATION PLAN

Practical application framework: The following implementation plan translates your narrative insights into structured action. This isn't just a conceptual exercise—it's a practical approach to embodying your new stories through daily practices and conscious choices. Choose one narrative to begin with, focusing on consistency rather than trying to revise multiple stories simultaneously.

Thirty-Day Story Revision Protocol

A. **Choose Your Focus Area**

- Which pillar needs immediate narrative revision?
- What specific story needs transformation?
- How will revising this story create movement?

B. **Develop Your Revision Strategy**

- Current limiting narrative:
- Alternative empowering narrative:
- Evidence supporting new narrative:
- Potential challenges to embodying new narrative:
- Support systems for narrative transition:

C. **Daily Implementation Practices**

- Morning narrative rehearsal (two to three minutes)
- Midday narrative check-in (one minute)
- Evening narrative reflection (five minutes)
- Weekly narrative review and adjustment (fifteen minutes)

D. **Story Integration Framework**

- Movement practices that embody new narrative:
- Language patterns that reinforce new narrative:
- Environmental cues that support transformation:
- Relationship dynamics that strengthen new narrative:

Comprehensive Narrative Revision Assessment

Consider your own journey of transformation.

Story Assessment

1. How might your current restrictions contain wisdom?
2. What failures have actually been redirections?
3. Where might your struggles offer value to others?

Movement Creation

1. What new patterns are waiting to emerge?
2. How could your challenges serve others?
3. Where might restriction become possibility?

Implementation Timeline

Time Frame	Narrative Focus	Specific Practice	Support Needed	Success Indicator
Weeks 1–2				
Weeks 3–4				
Weeks 5–8				
Weeks 9–12				

CHAPTER INTEGRATION: THE POWER OF NEW STORIES

Narrative revision is not about denying our past or fabricating a false future. It's about creating the right amount of space between what happened and how we carry it forward. Like the synovial fluid that allows for smooth joint movement, this space gives us freedom to move beyond our original limitations.

In this chapter, we've explored the following:

- How personal narratives shape our movement potential
- The process of identifying restrictive stories across all eight pillars
- Practical strategies for transforming limiting narratives
- Implementation frameworks for sustainable narrative revision

Key Chapter Takeaways

1. Your stories create the architecture of your movement.
2. Transformative events often create space for narrative revision.
3. Each life pillar has its own narrative structure.
4. Sustainable transformation requires both story revision and embodied practice.
5. Your greatest restrictions often contain the seeds of your unique contribution.

Your Immediate Next Steps

1. Complete the Narrative Assessment Framework for all eight pillars.
2. Identify the most restrictive narrative currently limiting your movement.
3. Create an alternative, empowering story using the Transformation Tool Kit.
4. Develop your Thirty-Day Story Revision Protocol.
5. Implement daily narrative revision practices.

Commitment moment: What one story will you begin rewriting today?

Old narrative:

New narrative:

First small action to embody this new story:

Support needed:

Remember: True transformation often comes not from escaping our restrictions but from transforming them into possibilities for yourself and others. The narrative revision work in this chapter provides the foundation for the edge exploration you'll undertake in chapter 4. As you begin to embody these new stories, you'll naturally find yourself ready to expand your boundaries and create movement in areas that previously felt restricted. Your revised narratives create the internal space that makes external movement possible.

In the next chapter, we'll explore how to consciously create new movement patterns that serve ourselves and the world around us.

FOUR

THE EDGE OF COMFORT

EXPANDING YOUR MOVEMENT BOUNDARIES

Who This Chapter Is For

- Professionals feeling stuck in their comfort zones
- Entrepreneurs seeking breakthrough performance
- Individuals ready to challenge personal limitations
- Anyone seeking to expand their capacity for growth

Key Transformational Outcomes

By the end of this chapter, you will be able to do the following:

- Understand the nature and purpose of comfort boundaries
- Learn to strategically push beyond limitations
- Develop techniques for building capacity through deliberate challenge
- Create sustainable frameworks for continuous expansion
- Build systems for turning restrictions into strengths

THE HIDDEN POTENTIAL OF LIMITATIONS

Our perceived limitations contain hidden gifts. Just as synovial spaces create possibility through defined boundaries, our life restrictions can become unexpected sources of strength. Many of us are resilient despite the obstacles we must face. We don't know why we press on, but we do instinctively. Acknowledging internal blessings just as much as external blessings can open up new channels of movement.

Reflection Point

What limitations have you been fighting against rather than working with?

How might your current challenges be hiding unexpected strengths?

When have restrictions actually created new possibilities in your life?

This chapter guides you through a systematic approach to boundary expansion—identifying your current edges, designing strategic challenges, and creating sustainable growth across all dimensions. Unlike random risk-taking or forced discomfort, this deliberate edge exploration creates optimal conditions for expanding your movement capacity in ways that align with your authentic self.

FINDING STRENGTH IN UNLIKELY COMBINATIONS

Our greatest potential often emerges where we least expect it—at the intersection of apparent contradictions. This truth revealed itself to me through many unlikely combinations: poor vision and basketball; busted limbs and kickboxing; color vision deficiency and IT infrastructure.

At IWG (Regus), I discovered that my inability to distinguish certain colors, traditionally considered essential for wiring, actually led me to develop superior organizational systems. I became so proficient at creating pristine, highly functional IT setups that the leadership tasked me with rescuing other general managers' chaotic server rooms—transforming disorganized spaces with wires dangling everywhere into meticulously ordered systems. By the time I completed each renovation, these IT rooms not only functioned flawlessly but provided an intuitive template for easily adding or removing clients in the business centers. This methodical approach contributed to my promotion to operations team lead for the Wall Street team of general managers. What began as a limitation transformed into specialized expertise precisely because I had to approach the challenge intently.

Key insight: Our greatest strengths often emerge from the most unexpected restrictions when we learn to work with rather than against our limitations.

THE VISION PARADOX: SEEING BEYOND SIGHT

At age fourteen, my vision was 20/200—I was legally blind without correction. My welfare glasses, broken at the nosepiece, caused more problems than they solved. Rather than face ridicule, I chose to navigate the world in a blur. This limitation would seem devastating for any young person attempting to play basketball, yet it taught me something profound about internal awareness.

Unable to wear my broken glasses during games, I learned to play basketball essentially blind. At first, this seemed impossible. But gradually, something remarkable emerged. Without clear visual input, my other senses heightened. My body developed an internal mapping system. I started landing shots on good players based purely on muscle memory and spatial awareness. At five feet nine inches tall, I even came within millimeters of dunking—all without being able to clearly see the rim, and while managing underlying joint pain.

Then came contact lenses, which were finally affordable through my afterschool high school job at the New York Public Library. Suddenly, I could see everything. Paradoxically, my game fell apart. The visual information interfered with my depth perception. I had to learn basketball all over again, this time integrating my newfound sight with my established internal navigation system.

The following assessment helps you reframe limitations as potential advantages. For each area of your life, identify both the conventional disadvantage and the hidden advantage it might contain. Then honestly evaluate how effectively you're currently utilizing this potential advantage, and develop a specific strategy for expanding its positive impact. This perspective shift is essential before beginning your edge exploration work, as it transforms your relationship with restrictions from seeing them as obstacles to overcome to approaching them as unique opportunities for differentiated growth. Remember that some of your greatest strengths may be hiding within what appears to be your most significant limitations.

Limitation Advantage Framework
Identify your potential "vision paradox" using this assessment.

Limitation	Conventional Disadvantage	Potential Hidden Advantage	Current Utilization (1–10)	Expansion Strategy
Physical				
Mental				
Emotional				
Spiritual				
Professional				
Relational				
Financial				
Purpose				

Coaching Moment: Internal Navigation

Consider your own experiences with limitation.

- What abilities have you developed because of, not despite, your challenges?
- Where might your perceived weaknesses actually be strengths?
- How have your restrictions forced you to develop deeper awareness?

MAPPING YOUR RESOURCES: BEYOND THE VISIBLE

Many of us overvalue external resources while we undervalue the internal capabilities we've developed through restriction. This resource-mapping framework helps you recognize both external and internal assets.

Comprehensive Resource Inventory
External Resources

Resource Category	Current Assets	Utilization Level (1–10)	Growth Potential	Next Development Step
Tools and Technology				
Financial Resources				
Formal Education				
Credentials				
Network Connections				

Internal Resources

Resource Category	Current Assets	Utilization Level (1–10)	Growth Potential	Next Development Step
Intuitive Knowledge				
Adaptability Skills				
Pattern Recognition				
Resilience Systems				
Creative Problem-Solving				

Integration Questions

- Which internal resources are you currently underutilizing?
- How might your past challenges have developed internal assets you don't recognize?
- What internal resources could compensate for external limitations?

Understanding both your external and internal resources provides the foundation for a more nuanced approach to movement. Rather than pursuing a single path forward, this resource awareness enables strategic development across multiple dimensions.

THE MULTIMOVEMENT PRINCIPLE: BEYOND THE "ONE THING"

Society often tells us to find our "one thing"—that singular passion or talent that defines us. But my journey with osteoarthritis and color vision deficiency taught me something different: Sometimes, our greatest strength comes from developing multiple centers of movement.

This multimovement approach addresses common challenges with singular identity.

- **Career tunnel syndrome:** When professional identity overshadows all other aspects of self.
- **One-dimensional success:** When a single metric determines one's entire sense of worth.
- **Purpose fixation:** The belief that we must discover one perfect calling.

Practical application: This mapping tool helps you identify current and potential centers of movement in your life. Rather than seeking a single "purpose," this framework helps you develop multiple areas of meaningful engagement. Complete this assessment to discover where you might expand beyond traditional single-focus approaches.

When rating the current engagement and joy factor, consider both the time invested and the emotional satisfaction derived from each domain. A high engagement with low joy indicates an area for potential adjustment. Then explore how these different domains might create unexpected synergies when developed in parallel rather than in isolation. This multidimensional approach creates both greater fulfillment and increased stability across your pillars of movement potential.

Multidimensional Capacity Framework
Map your current and potential movement centers.

Movement Domain	Current Engagement (1–10)	Joy Factor (1–10)	Growth Potential	Integration Opportunities
Primary Career				
Secondary Skills				
Creative Expression				
Physical Activities				
Intellectual Pursuits				
Relationship Roles				
Service Areas				
Spiritual Practices				

Integration Strategy

- Which domains could create unexpected synergies?
- How might developing multiple areas create more stability than focusing on one?
- What new domain would most balance your current movement patterns?

WHEN DREAMS SHIFT DIRECTION: THE ART OF ADAPTIVE PURPOSE

My military dreams in the delayed entry program hit a wall when my color vision deficiency and predispositions barred me from special operations or officer candidate school. So, too, were every one of my law enforcement goals at the highest levels.

Imagine telling young Kobe Bryant or Michael Jordan they had to coach instead of play—this is the reality tens of millions face annually. Whether through circumstances beyond our control or luck of the draw, our original paths often become unavailable to us.

Dream Redirection Protocol

When facing blocked paths, we have three choices.

1. **Fight against the limitation** (often leading to frustration).
2. **Give up entirely** (losing the core purpose).
3. **Find new ways to serve the same mission** (creating alternative movement).

This framework helps you navigate the crucial choice between fighting against limitations, abandoning your dreams entirely, or finding new expressions of your core purpose. Using the Mission Mapping Exercise below, identify a specific blocked dream or path, then carefully excavate the underlying values and purpose that made it meaningful to you. From this foundation, explore alternative expressions that might serve the same core mission through different means. This redirection process transforms dead ends into crossroads, allowing your deepest purpose to find new channels of expression rather than becoming trapped in rigid attachments to specific forms.

Mission Mapping Exercise

Blocked Dream	Core Purpose/Values	Alternative Expressions	Resources Needed	First Step

Redirection Questions

- What drives your original dream beyond the specific form?
- Which values underlie your goals?
- How else might these be expressed?
- What alternative paths might serve your purpose?
- How could your restrictions guide you to new possibilities?

CREATING VALUE THROUGH MULTIPLE CHANNELS: THE DIVERSIFICATION ADVANTAGE

My early restrictions taught me a vital lesson: Our worth extends far beyond our occupations. Who we are transcends social identities and daily patterns. What we can achieve is beyond profession or status. This understanding is particularly crucial in today's rapidly changing landscape where AI integration is transforming entire industries and career sectors are being dismantled overnight. The ability to adapt across multiple domains—to see yourself as more than your current role or expertise—has never been more essential. Because life dictated to me what I could and could not do from an early age, I had no choice but to be resilient in the face of that bias. My resilience led me to follow my interests in different fields and industries, creating a diverse skill portfolio that remains relevant regardless of technological disruption.

Ask yourself: If you were to be granted the opportunity to escape Earth's atmosphere on Jeff Bezos's Blue Origin rocket, you would likely find that most of your life's worries would fade to black in the infinite expanse of the universe. Your mindset would be forever changed as you were floating above the celestial body you call home, as noted by every astronaut who has taken similar leaps of collective faith. Why do you think it takes such extreme circumstances to unlock the fundamental truth popularized by the philosopher René Descartes, "I think, therefore I am?"

This framework helps you develop multiple pathways for creating value in the world rather than relying solely on your current methods. For each value channel, identify how you're currently expressing your contribution, then explore potential expansion opportunities that might leverage your existing capabilities in new contexts. Assess what additional resources you might need to develop these opportunities, and create a realistic implementation timeline. This expansion strategy increases your resilience in rapidly changing environments while allowing your unique gifts to reach different audiences through diverse expressions. The goal isn't to scatter your energy but to create an integrated ecosystem of contribution. This contribution could only be derived by the sum total of your individual life experiences.

Value Creation Expansion Strategy
Channel Mapping Exercise

Value Channel	Current Expression	Expansion Opportunity	Resources Needed	Implementation Timeline
Professional				
Creative				
Relational				
Community				
Knowledge				
Innovation				

Integration Questions

- How do your various experiences and strengths complement each other?
- Where might unexpected combinations create unique value?
- What new possibilities emerge from your diverse background?

THE EIGHT PILLARS IN ACTION: EXPANDING BOUNDARIES ACROSS DIMENSIONS

Our synovial spaces work together to create movement. Bones need space between themselves and other bones to move. Similarly, the Eight Pillars framework applies to creating movement through multiple channels.

In the following sections, we'll explore how to strategically expand boundaries in each pillar. For each dimension, we'll continue examining current beliefs and limitations, design experimental approaches, and create implementation pathways. As you work through these sections, notice which areas feel most restricted and which offer the most natural potential for expansion.

We begin our edge exploration with the most tangible dimension: physical movement. The principles you discover here will create a foundation for expanding boundaries in all other pillars.

1. Physical Movement: Beyond Limitations

With experience as a practitioner and manager of others in the healing arts, I've learned that while some people lie, our bodies don't. Many show up to a therapy session failing to disclose they've had reconstructive surgery on a joint. When joint mobility in a limb falls outside the average spectrum—whether restricted or hypermobile—an average manual therapist should pick up on this finding and document it.

We all harbor limitations across every aspect of our physical capacity, often concealed behind the veil of our self-perception. A client of mine once said, "My flat feet prevent me from running." I walked her through a basic biomechanical tour of her foot, showing her how to create the arch and how to resist directional isometric tension to slowly develop control of those muscles in different ranges. Because the mechanical structure of her foot appeared functional from a massage therapist's standpoint, I had her get an official diagnosis to see if the condition was structural, which would limit any improvement by strategic exercise. Her diagnosis came back with no structural damage.

She realized that the problem wasn't her feet but not enough time spent assessing, training, and treating her feet to use their full potential.

The pattern recognition exercise below helps you identify limiting beliefs about your physical capacity, examine their supporting evidence, consider contradicting evidence, and design specific experiments to test their validity. For each belief pattern, create an implementation plan that gradually and safely expands your movement boundaries. Remember that sustainable physical development comes not from dramatic challenges but from consistent exploration at the edges of your current capacity. This framework transforms your relationship with physical limitations from fixed barriers to evolving frontiers.

Physical Boundary Expansion Framework
Movement Pattern Recognition Exercise

Current Belief About Physical Capacity	Evidence Supporting	Evidence Contradicting	Expansion Experiment	Implementation Plan
"I can't ..."				
"My body always ..."				
"Because of my condition ..."				
"I'll never be able to ..."				

Adaptive Movement Protocol

A. **Baseline Capacity Assessment**

- Review your previous movement assessment to identify your current edge points.
- Note which movements trigger automatic compensation patterns.
- Identify situations where fear or caution (more than physical limitations) restricts movement.
- Connect these movement patterns to the underlying narratives you've documented.

B. **Edge Exploration Strategy**

- Choose one specific movement limitation you're ready to carefully expand.
- Create a progressive plan that increases the challenge by no more than 10 percent at each step.
- Establish clear criteria for distinguishing between productive discomfort and harmful pain.
- Design specific recovery practices to pair with each new movement challenge.

C. **Progress Documentation System**

- In a dedicated journal, record observations about movement quality and sensations.
- Conduct a structured reassessment of your movement capacity each week.
- Review and adjust your expansion approach monthly based on accumulated data.
- Plan larger movement goals and revise strategies quarterly for sustainable progress.

Physical edges can be strategically expanded just as your mental boundaries can be systematically developed. The flexibility you create in your thinking patterns enables movement across all other dimensions.

2. Mental Movement: Expanding Cognitive Boundaries

My time studying various methodologies of acting and working on projects revealed something crucial about mental patterns: Like muscles need various stimuli to grow, our minds require different forms of challenge to expand.

Learning stage combat, for instance, taught me that perception is reality. While watching two actors engage in stage combat for film, you'll quickly notice that the actors don't appear to be hitting each other on set. Far from it. But on film, every nuance of the actors blends with their positioning, timed movements, and focus of the lens to portray a believable altercation.

This mental flexibility addresses common thinking patterns that create restriction, including the following:

- **Binary thinking:** Reducing complex situations to either-or choices
- **Fixed mindset:** Seeing abilities as innate rather than developable
- **Cognitive fusion:** Treating thoughts as objective reality rather than subjective experience

Mental Boundary Expansion Tool Kit

Cognitive Flexibility Assessment
Rate your current flexibility in these mental domains (1–10).
(1 = highly rigid, 10 = optimally flexible)

- Perspective-taking ability:
- Comfort with uncertainty:
- Adaptability to new information:
- Tolerance for contradictions:
- Ability to hold multiple viewpoints:

Just as your physical edges can be strategically expanded, your mental boundaries can be systematically developed through deliberate practice. The following assessment helps you evaluate your current cognitive flexibility across various thinking dimensions and identify specific areas for growth, without needing to purchase a Blue Origin ticket. For each mental pattern, consider how it currently affects your choices, and explore alternative perspectives that might create new possibilities. Then design specific implementation methods that gradually expand your mental range without overwhelming your system. Remember that cognitive flexibility—like physical mobility— develops through consistent, progressive challenge rather than through occasional dramatic shifts.

Mental Edge Exploration Protocol

A. **Current Pattern Recognition**

- Select the most limiting mental pattern you identified in your previous assessment.
- Track specific moments when this pattern activates in your daily life.
- Note how this rigid thinking directly affects your decisions and physical movements.

B. **Boundary Expansion Exercise**

- Choose one long-standing belief you're ready to examine from different angles.
- Identify three perspectives that challenge your current thinking about this topic.
- Deliberately adopt each alternative viewpoint for a full day, noting how it changes your responses.
- Document both insights gained and internal resistance experienced with each perspective.

C. **Integration Practice**

- Incorporate a two-minute flexibility exercise into an existing daily routine.
- Create specific words or physical gestures that interrupt your habitual thought patterns.
- Practice deliberately shifting your viewpoints during ordinary conversations or meetings.
- Gradually increase the difficulty of cognitive challenges as your flexibility grows.

Mental Movement Mapping Matrix

Thinking Pattern	Current Boundary	Edge Exploration	Integration Method	Success Indicators
Analytical				
Creative				
Strategic				
Empathetic				
Intuitive				

As you develop mental flexibility, you naturally encounter your emotional edges. Expanding emotional range creates the capacity for both deeper experience and more authentic expression.

3. Emotional Movement: Creating Authentic Range

The evolution of my emotional expression—from activism to poetry at Nuyorican Poets Cafe—taught me that emotional movement needs both structure and freedom. Like a joint requires both stability and mobility, emotional health needs both containment and expression.

The Emotional Boundary Assessment that follows helps you map your current comfort level with various emotions, identify how you typically express them, and pinpoint specific edges where growth is possible. For each emotion, design a progressive strategy that gradually (one day at a time) expands your capacity for authentic experience and expression. This framework transforms emotional development from vague aspiration to deliberate practice, creating specific pathways for experiencing greater emotional range while maintaining appropriate boundaries and integration.

Emotional Range Expansion Framework
Emotional Boundary Assessment

Emotion	Current Comfort (1–10)	Expression Method	Expansion Edge	Growth Strategy
Joy/Excitement				
Anger/Frustration				
Sadness/Grief				
Fear/Anxiety				
Shame/Guilt				
Love/Connection				

Emotional Range Development Protocol

A. **Current Pattern Recognition**

- From your previous emotional assessment, select one emotion you consistently avoid or exaggerate.
- Pay attention to specific bodily sensations that accompany this emotion when it arises.
- Identify the exact circumstances that reliably trigger your habitual emotional response.

B. **Boundary Expansion Strategy**

- Choose one emotional response pattern you're ready to expand or modify.
- Design a step-by-step approach to gradually experience this emotion in increasingly challenging contexts.
- Develop specific practices for both appropriately containing and authentically expressing this emotion.
- Create a personalized recovery ritual to use after emotionally challenging experiences.

C. **Integration Framework**

- Incorporate a brief emotional check-in during an existing daily routine rather than creating a separate practice.
- Designate one specific day each week to deliberately work with your chosen emotional edge.
- Use your monthly review session to assess how your emotional range is expanding across different contexts.
- Adjust your emotional development plan quarterly based on progress and emerging challenges.

Application Questions

- Where do you perform emotions rather than move through them?
- How might emotional patterns be limiting your growth?
- What new forms of expression could create movement?

Your emotional expansion naturally leads to deeper questions of meaning and purpose. Spiritual boundary exploration addresses how you connect with what matters most amid life's inevitable constraints.

4. Spiritual Movement: Finding Purpose in Restriction

My battle with faith over two decades revealed something profound about spiritual movement: Like physical rehabilitation, it requires both patience and progressive development. Matthew 6:26 offers a reminder that even birds are provided for. This speaks to a deeper truth: Sometimes, our greatest growth happens not through striving but through surrendering to deeper wisdom.

Our spiritual boundaries—how we connect with meaning, purpose, and values that transcend immediate experience—can also be intentionally expanded. The following assessment helps you evaluate your current comfort level with various spiritual dimensions and identify specific growth edges. For each spiritual aspect, map your current practices, note where your comfort zone ends, and design strategic approaches to explore beyond these familiar territories. This framework helps make spiritual growth concrete and practical rather than abstract, creating measurable progress in what might otherwise remain conceptual territory.

Spiritual Expansion Tool Kit

Purpose Boundary Assessment

Spiritual Dimension	Current Practice	Comfort Zone Edge	Expansion Opportunity	Growth Strategy
Purpose/Meaning				
Faith/Trust				
Connection/Oneness				
Values/Ethics				
Transcendence/Wonder				

Spiritual Edge Exploration Protocol

A. **Current Pattern Recognition**

- Identify which spiritual practice from your existing routine has become mechanical rather than meaningful.
- Consider which spiritual questions you've been avoiding or setting aside.
- Review how your current spiritual boundaries affect other dimensions of your life.

B. **Boundary Expansion Strategy**

- Choose one aspect of your spiritual understanding you're ready to examine more deeply.
- Create a progressive approach to exploring this area through increasingly challenging practices.
- Develop specific questions that probe beneath surface-level understanding.
- Find practical ways to integrate these new spiritual insights into daily decisions.

C. **Integration Framework**

- Connect your spiritual awareness to an existing daily touchpoint rather than adding a separate practice.
- Designate one weekly opportunity to intentionally explore your spiritual edge.
- During your monthly review, evaluate how your spiritual understanding is evolving.
- Each quarter, reassess your spiritual growth trajectory and adjust your exploration accordingly.

Spiritual Movement Questions

- How does your sense of purpose create movement, and where does it limit movement?
- Where might rigid beliefs be restricting natural growth?
- What practices create sustainable spiritual development?

The clarity that emerges from spiritual exploration naturally extends to how you express yourself professionally. Expanding professional boundaries allows you to create value in more diverse and meaningful ways.

5. Professional Movement: Creating Multiple Impacts

Managing more than 180 team members at Planned Companies taught me that professional movement isn't just about climbing ladders—it's about creating ripple effects. Like synovial joints that move through various planes, healthy careers often move through unexpected shifts and adaptations.

Your professional expression offers rich opportunities for strategic boundary expansion. This assessment helps you identify specific professional dimensions where growth would create meaningful impact, evaluate your current comfort level, and design targeted approaches for development. For each area, consider what resources you'll need, and then create a realistic implementation strategy. This framework transforms professional growth from generic advancement to strategic capacity expansion, focusing on developing capabilities that align with your authentic strengths and create genuine value for others rather than simply pursuing conventional career paths.

Professional Boundary Expansion Framework
Career Edge Assessment

Professional Dimension	Current Comfort (1-10)	Edge Opportunity	Resources Needed	Growth Strategy
Technical Skills				
Leadership Capacity				
Innovation/Creativity				
Strategic Thinking				
Relationship Building				
Communication Range				

Professional Edge Exploration Protocol

A. Current Pattern Recognition

- From your earlier assessment, select one professional area where you consistently stay within your comfort zone.
- Identify a previously valuable skill that hasn't significantly improved in the past year.
- Consider how your current professional boundaries might be limiting growth in other life dimensions.

B. Boundary Expansion Strategy

- Choose one specific professional capability you're ready to deliberately expand.
- Design a sequence of increasingly challenging projects that gradually stretch this capability.
- Identify mentors, resources, or learning opportunities needed to support this expansion.
- Develop a method for applying these emerging skills in your current role.

C. Career Expansion Road Map

- Focus intensively on developing one specific skill or capability for the next thirty days.
- Create a ninety-day plan that builds your expertise across a complementary set of professional abilities.
- Develop a six-month strategy for transforming how you approach your field or industry.
- Design a twelve-month framework for evolving your professional identity and impact.

Professional Evolution Questions

- How does your current role enable growth, and how does it restrict growth?
- Where might lateral movement create new possibilities?
- What professional patterns have you outgrown?

How you navigate professional contexts connects directly to how you interact with your broader environments. Environmental edge exploration examines how you can create more intentional and adaptive relationships with the spaces you inhabit.

6. Relational Movement: Connecting with Authenticity

Like the coordinated movements of joints, authentic relationships require both connection and appropriate space to function optimally. Your relational boundaries—how you engage with others, what you share, and how you maintain autonomy while creating intimacy—significantly impact your capacity for meaningful connection.

Relational edge expansion involves moving toward whichever you typically avoid: deeper vulnerability if you tend toward distance, clearer boundaries if you tend toward fusion, or genuine asking if you tend toward self-sufficiency.

My relational patterns emerged from early lessons about connection and absence. I didn't grow up with my biological father. My stepfather, though physically present, was emotionally absent during my formative years—his love and attention were reserved for his biological son, my brother. What grounded me wasn't family connection. It was music, books, sports, and stories of resilience in Aesop's fables (and in other characters who endured, adapted, and found meaning despite their circumstances).

But my relational self-consciousness had another source: My body kept betraying me. Friends constantly teased me about getting injured—again. I developed a pattern of constantly questioning myself. Why did people interpret me in ways that didn't match my truth? Were they seeing something I couldn't? I became hypervigilant about how I was being perceived. I was simultaneously self-conscious and awkwardly confident in my abilities; hesitantly confident. I internalized everything, endlessly analyzed interactions, and tried to understand the gap between how I experienced myself and how others seemed to experience me.

That analytical pattern—the one that makes this book heavy on frameworks and assessment tools—didn't emerge from my intellectual preference. It emerged from relational necessity. If I couldn't trust my body or count on consistent family connection, I could at least try to understand the patterns. Analyzing became my way of creating stability.

I learned that relationships couldn't be counted on for stability—but stories, music, self-reliance, and understanding systems could be. That pattern carried forward connection through ideas rather than vulnerability, self-sufficiency instead of interdependence, and analyzing instead of feeling.

When osteoarthritis further plagued my physical capacity as an adult with intense pain, my internalization pattern intensified. I learned to put on a show—to move through the world as if I wasn't hurting. I thought I was protecting others from my limitations, maintaining independence, and avoiding the vulnerability I'd learned early on wasn't safe.

And it wasn't safe—not originally. Because I grew up in an impoverished area, I quickly learned that exposing weakness was dangerous. Showing pain invited exploitation. Appearing vulnerable made me a target. The stern exterior, the controlled presentation, and the refusal to let anyone see me hurt weren't neurotic tendencies. They were survival strategies. They kept me safe when my safety wasn't guaranteed.

But the mask I created for protection had unintended consequences when the context changed. Hiding pain required that stern, controlled exterior even in relationships where I was no longer in danger. What I intended as strength appeared as coldness. Distance. Aloofness. I was protecting people from seeing my pain, but they were experiencing me as someone who was emotionally unreachable. The survival strategy that had served me in one environment became the barrier to connection in another.

My relationships had to adapt in ways I'd been avoiding my entire life. I couldn't sustain the facade when my pain demanded help. I couldn't hide behind self-sufficiency when my body forced dependence. My wife learned to read my nonverbal cues—not the manufactured calm, but the actual signals beneath it. She could tell when I was hurting, even when I said I was fine. That forced me into a different kind of presence than I'd experienced when I was growing up: being known even when I didn't want to be seen.

And still, today, the pattern persists. I'm at a party, engaging in conversation, and I feel it starting: My body begins to seize, and my joints lock up like I'm the Tin Man in need of oil. The pain intensifies to the point where I know I'm minutes from being on the floor in visible agony. So I exit. Stage left. Quickly. Before anyone can see me in that state. I tell myself I'm being considerate—that I don't want to make others uncomfortable. But I know the truth: I'm still protecting myself from being fully seen in my limitation. I'm still choosing isolation over vulnerable presence.

Having relational capacity isn't about being perfectly emotionally articulate or physically expressive. It's about finding authentic connection within the capacities you have—and being willing to stretch those edges incrementally over time. I'm still learning this. My edge is still letting people stay when my body breaks down. Yours will be different but equally uncomfortable.

I'm not sharing this to receive sympathy—I'm sharing it because the work I'm asking you to do requires the same honesty I'm practicing. Identifying your relational edge means acknowledging where you're still protecting yourself, even when those protective measures cost you connection. My edge involves physical limitation that forces relational vulnerability. Yours might have nothing to do with physical pain. But the pattern is universal: We each have relational moves we avoid and protective strategies we've maintained for so long that they feel like our identity rather than choices we make.

The question isn't whether you have an edge—you do. The question is whether you're willing to see it clearly enough to expand it.

So where is your edge? Most people know instinctively—it's the relational move that feels uncomfortable, the one you've been avoiding, the pattern you've maintained for so long that it feels like your identity rather than a choice. The list below isn't comprehensive, but it captures common edges. As you read through them, notice which ones create resistance. That resistance often points directly to your growth opportunity.

Relational Edge Identification

Common relational edges involve moving from restricted patterns toward more authentic engagement, such as the following:

- From avoiding vulnerability to sharing one authentic feeling
- From having weak boundaries to saying no once this week
- From never asking for help to requesting support one time
- From avoiding conflict to directly addressing one small issue
- From staying surface-level to going deeper in one conversation
- From isolating to having one coffee with a potential friend
- From people-pleasing to expressing your actual preference once
- From over-functioning to letting someone else handle something

Identifying your edge is one thing. Actually expanding it requires structure. Without a framework, good intentions dissolve into avoidance. The tool kit below breaks edge expansion into manageable steps—not because the work is easy, but because making it systematic increases the likelihood that you'll actually do it.

Relational Expansion Tool Kit

Use the following frameworks to systematically expand your relational edge.

A. **Identify Your Relational Pattern**

- Do you tend toward over-connection (fusion, enmeshment, or weak boundaries) or under-connection (distance, isolation, rigid boundaries)?
- Where do you consistently play a similar role across different relationships?
- What protective patterns did you develop in your early relationships that you're still using?

B. **Design Your 10 Percent Expansion**

- If you avoid vulnerability, share one struggle with a trusted person this week.
- If you have weak boundaries, say no to one request that doesn't serve you.
- If you never ask for help, request assistance with one small thing.
- If you avoid conflict, directly address one small disagreement.

C. **Prepare for Response Variations**

Relational edge expansion involves risk because you cannot control others' responses. Prepare yourself for the following:

- You might be vulnerable with someone and then be rejected.
- You might set boundaries and face conflict.
- You might ask for help and be told no.
- You might address an issue and create temporary discomfort.

The goal isn't to guarantee others' behavior. It's to increase your capacity to show up authentically regardless of their responses. Understanding the framework helps. But understanding doesn't equal practice. The protocol below creates a twenty-one-day structure for actually expanding your relational edge—not through dramatic transformation, but through consistent, small experiments that build new capacity over time.

Relational Edge Exploration Protocol

This twenty-one-day framework helps you expand your relational edge systematically.

Week One: Pattern Observation

- Notice your typical relational moves. (How do you create distance? How do you manage conflict? When do you hide versus reveal yourself?)
- Document similar patterns across different relationships.
- Identify your primary relational edge.

Week Two: Micro-Expansion Practice

- Choose one small relational edge to expand.
- Practice a tiny version three times this week.
- Notice your internal experience and others' responses.

Week Three: Sustained Expansion

- Increase the frequency or depth of your edge practice.
- Navigate any discomfort that arises.
- Reflect on what became possible through expansion.

The twenty-one-day protocol gives you the process. But tracking your specific journey—your particular edge, your unique challenges, and your individual progress—requires documentation. The framework below helps you name what you're working with and monitor what's shifting.

Relational Boundary Expansion Framework

Track your relational edge expansion.

Connection Pattern Assessment

- Current relational edge:
- Situations that trigger protective patterns:
- Relationships where you're most authentic:
- Relationships where you're most guarded:

Boundary Expansion Strategy

- Specific edge to practice:
- 10 percent expansion this week:
- Support person:
- Recovery practice after expansion:

Before you can effectively expand your edge, you need clarity about where you actually are. The questions below aren't redundant with earlier frameworks—they're designed to help you get specific about your current relational reality. Answer them after you've spent time observing your patterns, not before.

Authentic Connection Assessment

Evaluate your current relational patterns.

- Where do you tend toward over-connection (insufficient boundaries)?
- Where do you maintain excessive distance (insufficient connection)?
- In which relationships do you feel most authentic?
- What situations trigger your protective patterns?
- What small relational experiment would expand your comfort zone without overwhelming your system?

This assessment identifies where you are. But transformation requires vision—the ability to imagine what might become possible if you expand your edge. The questions below help you move from describing your current state to envisioning what could shift. They're not about finding "right" answers. They're about opening your mind to think about what your strategic expansion might create.

Relational Expansion Questions

- How might strategic vulnerability create more meaningful connections?
- Where could having clearer boundaries actually improve the quality of your relationships?
- What relationship pattern, if shifted, would create more authenticity?
- Which edge would serve your relational growth most: deeper connection or clearer boundaries?

Remember: Relational development isn't about becoming someone different. It's about showing up more authentically as yourself—which paradoxically often requires moving beyond patterns you developed to protect yourself. Your edge isn't where you're broken. It's where your next growth lives.

---

7. Financial Movement: Creating Room for Resource Flow

Just as a joint needs proper support to move freely, our financial lives require balance between structure and flexibility. This balance allows for optimal resource flow and adaptation to changing circumstances.

Your relationship with resources—including money, time, and energy—represents another dimension for strategic boundary expansion. This framework helps you assess your current comfort level with various financial aspects and identify specific edges where growth would create meaningful movement. For each dimension, explore possibilities for expansion, identify necessary resources, and design a practical implementation strategy. This approach transforms financial development from abstract goals into concrete practices that gradually expand your capacity for resource management. Remember that financial flexibility often creates space in multiple other life dimensions when approached with intention and alignment.

Financial Boundary Expansion Framework

Financial Dimension	Current Comfort (1–10)	Expansion Edge	Resources Needed	Growth Strategy
Income Diversity				
Vulnerability				
Risk Tolerance				
Resource Allocation				
Abundance Mindset				

Financial Edge Exploration Protocol

A. **Current Pattern Recognition**

- From your financial assessment, identify one specific area where you consistently avoid financial decisions.
- Select a limiting financial belief you discovered that most restricts your movement potential.
- Consider which inherited family pattern around money continues to influence your resource management.

B. **Boundary Expansion Strategy**

- Choose one financial boundary you're ready to carefully expand.
- Create a step-by-step approach that gradually increases financial challenge or responsibility.
- Establish specific risk management measures that make this exploration feel secure.
- Develop ways to connect this financial growth with other pillars in your life.

C. **Implementation Framework**

- Design a thirty-day financial experiment that tests a new approach to resources.
- Establish a consistent weekly check-in to capture insights and adjust your approach.
- Create a method for integrating financial learnings into your overall system.
- Develop criteria for selecting your next financial edge once this exploration is complete.

Through my experience transitioning from Wall Street to entrepreneurship after 9/11, I discovered that financial flexibility isn't just about how much money we have—it's about creating the right relationship with our resources. Just as a well-calibrated joint needs both stability and mobility, financial health requires both structure and adaptability.

The pandemic revealed this truth on a global scale, as I observed the contrasting approaches of companies like WeWork and IWG (Regus). Both faced unprecedented challenges, but those who had created appropriate financial spaces—maintaining reserves, developing multiple revenue streams, and structuring debt responsibly—had significantly more flexibility to adapt and evolve.

Financial Resilience Framework
Rate your current flexibility in these financial domains (1–10).
(1 = highly rigid, 10 = optimally flexible)

- Income source diversity:
- Emergency fund adequacy:
- Debt structure flexibility:
- Spending pattern adaptability:
- Investment approach balance:

Financial Expansion Questions

- Where could more flexibility create greater security?
- What small financial experiments might expand your comfort zone?
- How might your relationship with money reflect deeper values?
- Where are you trading long-term movement for short-term comfort?
- What financial edges, if expanded, would create the most freedom?

Your approach to resources influences how you connect with others. Social edge exploration examines how you can create more authentic and meaningful relationships while honoring appropriate boundaries.

8. Purpose Movement: Finding Meaning in Restriction

Your edge with purpose often lies not in finding some grand calling but in recognizing the meaning that is already present in your life—and having the courage to honor it. Identifying your purpose edges involves moving from waiting for perfect clarity to acting on what matters now, from dismissing small significance to recognizing quiet impact, and from searching for purpose "out there" to creating it through how you live.

For years, I waited for my "real" purpose to reveal itself. I accomplished things—built careers in hospitality, massage therapy, personal training, and real estate—but I carried the sense that these were just placeholders until I discovered my true calling. This waiting narrative prevented me from fully investing in what I was actually doing, and it kept me from recognizing the meaning that was already present in how I was helping others move better, think more clearly, and live with less restriction.

The edge came when I stopped searching and started recognizing that my purpose wasn't something separate from my limitations. It emerged directly from them. Every physical challenge taught me something about creating movement within constraints. Every blocked path revealed an alternative route. Every restriction became material for understanding how I could help others navigate their own limitations.

That recognition—that my restriction *is* my purpose—transformed everything. Not because it eliminated my challenges but because it revealed that they weren't obstacles to overcome before I could begin living purposefully. They were the very things clarifying what I'm here to contribute.

Purpose Edge Identification

Common ways to identify purpose edges involve moving from restricted patterns toward more expansive engagement with meaning.

- From waiting for clarity to making one purposeful choice this week
- From avoiding commitment to committing to one meaningful project
- From thinking small to articulating a larger vision (even privately)
- From dreaming big but not acting to taking one small implementation step
- From hiding your contribution to sharing your work with one person
- From waiting for perfect conditions to starting with what you have now
- From dismissing daily meaning to documenting small significance

Purpose Expansion Tool Kit

Use these frameworks to systematically expand your purpose edge.

A. **Identify Your Current Purpose Edge**

- Where does your sense of purpose feel most restricted?
- What keeps you from engaging more fully with what matters?
- What small expansion would create more alignment between your values and your life?

B. **Design Your 10 Percent Expansion**

- If you currently avoid purpose work entirely, spend fifteen minutes this week reflecting on what matters most.
- If you wait for clarity, take one action that is aligned with your values this week.
- If you keep your purpose private, share one aspect of what matters to you with someone you trust.
- If you dream but don't act, take the smallest possible step toward meaningful work.

C. **Create Your Recovery Protocol**

Purpose work—even in small doses—can feel vulnerable. Build in recovery in the following ways:

- After you make a meaningful contribution, acknowledge what you created.
- After you take a values-aligned action, document the experience.
- After you take a purposeful risk, process the emotions that arise.
- After you engage in significant meaning-making, rest before expanding further.

Purpose Edge Exploration Protocol

This twenty-one-day framework helps you systematically expand your purpose edge.

Week One: Awareness Practice

- **Daily:** Notice moments of meaning (even small ones).
- **Document:** What created genuine significance today?
- **Observe:** When do you dismiss or overlook purpose?

Week Two: Small Action Practice

- **Daily:** Take one action that is aligned with your values.
- **Notice:** How do small, purposeful choices affect your sense of meaning?
- **Experiment:** Try different ways of creating contribution.

Week Three: Edge Expansion Practice

- **Challenge:** Move beyond your current purpose comfort zone.
- **Action:** Share something meaningful with someone.
- **Reflect:** What became possible through expansion?

Purpose Transformation Road Map

Track your purpose expansion over time.

- Current purpose edge:
- First 10 percent expansion:
- Evidence of progress:
- Next expansion:
- Support needed:

Purpose Movement Questions

Reflect on these questions as you expand your purpose edge.

- What meaning already exists in your life that you've been dismissing?
- How might your current limitations clarify rather than obscure your purpose?
- What would change if you stopped searching for purpose and started creating it?
- What small action could you take today that is aligned with your values?
- How does your unique combination of experiences position you to contribute something specific?

Remember: Purpose doesn't require grand gestures or perfect clarity. It emerges through showing up authentically with the capacity you have, contributing what you can within your current constraints, and paying attention to what creates genuine meaning. Your edge isn't about becoming someone different. It's about honoring who you already are and what you're actually here to do.

AUTHENTIC CONNECTION ASSESSMENT

Evaluate your current social patterns.

- Where do you tend toward over-connection (insufficient boundaries)?
- Where do you maintain excessive distance (insufficient connection)?
- In which relationships do you feel most authentic?
- What social situations trigger protective patterns?
- What small edge expansions would create more authentic connection?

Social Expansion Questions

- How might strategic vulnerability create more meaningful connections?
- Where could clearer boundaries actually improve the quality of your relationships?
- What relationship patterns, if shifted, would create more authenticity?
- How do your current social circles expand your overall movement, and how do they limit your overall movement?
- What small social experiments would expand your comfort zone without overwhelming your system?

FINDING YOUR EDGE: THE BOXING LESSON

Just when I thought I understood my edge of comfort, 2023 offered another lesson. Life came full circle when my daughter began showing interest in boxing—a sport I had been intimately involved with in my youth. Wanting to help her and others avoid needless injuries, I obtained USA Boxing green-level, then bronze-level, certifications and level one official status. I trained with Olympic team coaches and began timekeeping and judging in my local boxing club (Local Boxing Club 44).

What began as a father's desire to share knowledge quickly reignited my own passion. The opportunity to merge my past experience with my evolving manual therapy expertise felt like the perfect way to guide my daughter while honoring my own journey with the sport.

Then came the moment when I decided to lead by example—a decision that would teach me a profound lesson about edges. The training bug struck again, and I wanted to get in the ring; to show rather than just tell. A sparring session with a marine twenty-five years my junior revealed something crucial about limitations: Sometimes, the edge isn't where we think it is.

The instant the bell rang, an ossification in my left hip was triggered, and nerves in my thoracic and lumbar spine were damaged by a quick movement. My ability to properly move vanished, leaving me defenseless. Driven by ego and encouraged by the referee, I pushed past my true edge through four rounds. My face showed the physical toll, but the deeper consequence was my inability to flex or rotate my left femur without agony.

Key implementation tool: This framework helps you distinguish between productive challenges that create growth and potentially hazardous boundaries that could cause harm. Before pushing any edge, use this assessment to evaluate whether it represents an appropriate growth opportunity or a risk that requires a different approach.

This framework prevents the common pitfalls of either avoiding all edges (limiting growth) or pushing past important protective boundaries (risking harm). The goal is strategic, sustainable expansion rather than reckless risk-taking.

Edge Identification Framework
Distinguishing Productive Edges from Hazardous Boundaries

Domain	Productive Edge Characteristics	Hazardous Boundary Signs	Personal Assessment	Edge Approach Strategy
Physical	Appropriate challenge, recovery possible	Pain, risk of injury, poor form		
Mental	Stretching understanding, productive confusion	Overwhelm, shutdown, anxiety		
Emotional	Growth discomfort, controlled vulnerability	Trauma trigger, flooding, shutdown		
Spiritual	Meaningful questioning, expanded awareness	Existential crisis, disconnection		
Professional	Skill stretch, supported challenge	Risk of burnout, ethical compromise		
Relational	Authentic vulnerability, mutual growth	Boundary violation, manipulation		
Financial	Calculated risk, managed uncertainty	Survival threat, irrational gamble		
Purpose	Living into meaningful contribution	Purpose martyrdom, existential burnout		

Edge Recognition Questions

- Where might your perceived limitations be protecting you?
- How could stepping back actually increase your long-term impact?
- What wisdom have your challenges prepared you to share?
- What's the difference between courage and ego in your current edge exploration?

THE DELIBERATE EDGE PROTOCOL: STRATEGIC BOUNDARY EXPANSION

Effective growth happens not by randomly pushing all boundaries but through deliberate, strategic edge exploration. This framework helps you approach your edges with precision and wisdom.

The following twenty-one-day process provides a complete framework for intentional boundary expansion. Rather than attempting to change everything at once, this protocol helps you select specific edges to explore, design appropriate challenges, monitor responses, and integrate learnings. This systematic approach creates sustainable growth without the burnout often associated with pushing too many boundaries simultaneously. Use this process for any edge you've identified as both meaningful and appropriate for development.

Twenty-One-Day Edge Exploration Process

Phase 1: Assessment (Days 1–3)

1. **Select your focus pillar:** Choose the dimension that showed the greatest potential for growth in your comprehensive assessment.
2. **Identify your current comfortable capacity:** Determine what you can consistently do without strain in this area.
3. **Map the perceived edge boundary:** Note the specific point where you begin to feel significant resistance or discomfort.
4. **Define minimum effective challenge (10 percent beyond comfort):** Calculate a precise increment that creates growth without overwhelming your system.
5. **Design your recovery protocol:** Create specific practices to implement after each edge exploration session.

Phase 2: Exploration (Days 4–17)

1. **Daily Edge Approach Practice**

- **Morning preparation ritual:** Perform a five-minute centering practice that prepares your mind and body for boundary expansion.
- **Edge exploration activity:** Engage in your chosen challenge for a predetermined time period, noting sensations as they arise.
- **Postexploration recovery practice:** Immediately implement your designed recovery protocol to integrate the experience.
- **Evening reflection and documentation:** Record specific observations about your responses, resistance points, and insights.

2. **Implementation Tracking**

Day	Edge Activity	Response (1–10)	Insights	Adjustments Needed
4				
5				
12				
17				

Phase 3: Integration (Days 18–21)

A. **Comprehensive Assessment**

- **Initial capacity versus current capacity:** Measure specific changes in your capacity compared to your day-one baseline.
- **Key insights gained:** Identify the three most significant learnings about your response to edge exploration.
- **Unexpected discoveries:** Note surprising developments or responses that weren't anticipated.
- **New edge awareness:** Document how your perception of your boundaries has shifted through this process.

B. **Sustainability Design**

- **Optimal challenge level identified:** Determine the precise degree of challenge that creates growth without depletion.
- **Ideal recovery protocol:** Refine your recovery approach based on what proved most effective during the exploration phase.
- **Integration into your regular routine:** Design a maintainable practice that continues your growth while fitting into your life.
- **Next edge to explore:** Select your next boundary expansion focus based on insights from this process.

Practical Edge Exploration Tools

While the twenty-one-day protocol provides the overall structure for edge exploration, the following tools offer specific implementation strategies. Each addresses a different aspect of boundary expansion, from determining appropriate challenge levels to creating support systems.

1. The 10 Percent Rule: Systematic Edge Expansion

Sustainable growth happens through consistent, incremental challenge. The 10 Percent Rule provides a framework for boundary expansion without burnout.

10 Percent Edge Expansion Protocol

A. **Establish your current baseline capacity in your chosen domain.**

B. **Calculate your 10 percent challenge increment.**

- Current capacity:
- 10 percent increment:
- Target edge challenge:

C. **Design your progressive expansion plan.**

Week	Target Challenge	Support Required	Recovery Protocol	Success Indicators
1				
2				
3				
4				

2. The Edge Recovery Balance: Sustainable Growth

Effective boundary expansion requires balancing challenge with recovery. This framework helps you design optimal recovery protocols based on the intensity of your edge exploration. For each level of challenge, the table provides recommended recovery ratios and suggests activities that support integration and restoration. Use this structure to create your personalized recovery approach tailored to your specific edge exploration. Remember that recovery isn't an optional luxury but an essential component of sustainable growth—the more significant the challenge, the more deliberate your restoration practices must be.

Edge Recovery Balancing Framework

Challenge Intensity (1–10)	Recommended Recovery Ratio	Recovery Activities	Implementation Strategy
1–3 (Mild)	1:1 (equal time)		
4–6 (Moderate)	1:2 (double time)		
7–8 (Significant)	1:3 (triple time)		
9–10 (Maximum)	1:5 (five times)		

Personalized Recovery Protocol

A. **Primary edge exploration:**
B. **Challenge intensity (1–10):**
C. **Optimal recovery ratio:**
D. **Recovery activities:**

- Physical:
- Mental:
- Emotional:
- Relational:

3. The Wisdom Council: Edge Exploration Support

Strategic boundary expansion often requires external perspective and support. This framework helps you assemble a personalized "wisdom council" for your edge exploration journey. For each support role, identify a specific person whose expertise or perspective would benefit your growth, determine exactly how they'll assist you, and establish clear methods for engagement. This intentional network creates both accountability and encouragement while providing essential feedback and perspective that might not be available through self-assessment alone. The goal isn't dependency but rather enhanced awareness and strategic guidance.

Edge Guidance Network Design

Support Role	Person	Specific Expertise	How They'll Help	Engagement Method
Technical Expert				
Emotional Support				
Perspective Challenger				
Recovery Guide				
Accountability Partner				

Implementation Strategy

- Establish a specific format for engaging with your support network, such as monthly video calls, weekly text updates, or dedicated review sessions.

- Create a consistent calendar for connecting with each council member, with clear agenda items and time boundaries for efficient exchanges.

- Develop targeted questions for each adviser based on their unique expertise rather than asking for general feedback.

- Design a systematic approach for evaluating, prioritizing, and incorporating the counsel you receive into your practice.

INTEGRATION: CREATING SUSTAINABLE MOVEMENT

Understanding how these eight pillars interact creates the foundation for transformative change. Just as a healthy joint moves through multiple planes, a fulfilled life requires movement through multiple channels of expression. When we align our environments with deeper purpose, what initially appears as restriction often becomes the catalyst for profound growth.

The individual tools and pillar-specific approaches we've explored now come together in a unified strategy for boundary expansion. This integration creates a balanced approach that addresses multiple dimensions while maintaining focus and preventing overwhelm.

It's important to recognize that perfect balance across all eight pillars is neither realistic nor necessary. Life naturally creates seasons when certain dimensions receive more attention while others temporarily recede. The goal isn't to maintain perpetual homeostasis—which would itself become a form of rigidity—but rather to develop the awareness to recognize when imbalances begin to create negative impacts. By understanding which pillars currently need attention and which are providing strength, you can strategically direct your resources where they'll create the most significant movement for your entire system.

Now that you've explored specific boundaries across all eight pillars, this integration framework helps you create a unified strategy for the next ninety days. Rather than attempting to expand all boundaries simultaneously, this approach guides you to select three primary focus areas and develop a progressive implementation plan. For each month, identify your primary focus, specific edge activities, necessary support systems, and clear success indicators. This balanced approach addresses multiple dimensions while maintaining focus and preventing overwhelm, creating sustainable momentum toward your most meaningful growth edges.

Comprehensive Edge Exploration Plan

Select your primary focus pillars for the next ninety days.

1. Primary pillar:
2. Secondary pillar:
3. Support pillar:

Ninety-Day Edge Exploration Strategy

Month	Primary Focus	Edge Activities	Support System	Success Indicators
Month 1				
Month 2				
Month 3				

Integration Strategy

- Incorporate one specific Boundary Expansion Exercise into an existing daily routine to ensure consistent implementation.

- Set aside twenty to thirty minutes on the same day each week to evaluate which edges are creating growth and which need adjustment.

- Conduct a comprehensive review of all eight pillars to identify where new edges have emerged and where previous boundaries have expanded.

- Maintain regular contact with specific individuals who understand your growth journey and can provide perspective when you reach challenging edges.

Personalization point: The following exercise helps you create your own philosophy of boundary expansion—a personalized approach that honors your unique limitations, strengths, and growth edges. This manifesto serves as both a compass for decision-making and a reminder of your commitment to deliberate growth.

FINAL INTEGRATION EXERCISE: YOUR PERSONAL EDGE MANIFESTO

Take a moment to craft your personal philosophy of boundary expansion.

1. My definition of a healthy edge is:
2. I commit to approaching my edges with:
3. I will know I'm at a productive edge when:
4. I will recognize a hazardous boundary when:
5. My support system for edge exploration includes:

6. My recovery protocol will consist of:
7. I will measure growth through:
8. My first edge exploration will be:

Key Chapter Takeaways

1. Limitations often contain hidden strengths when approached strategically.
2. Strategic edge exploration requires both challenge and recovery.
3. The 10 Percent Rule provides a framework for sustainable boundary expansion.
4. Truly knowing your edges requires honest self-assessment.
5. Multidimensional development creates more resilient growth than single-focus approaches.
6. Support systems are essential for effective boundary expansion.

Your Immediate Next Steps

1. Complete the edge identification frameworks for all eight pillars.
2. Select your primary focus for boundary expansion.
3. Design your Twenty-One-Day Edge Exploration Process.
4. Assemble your edge guidance network.
5. Implement your first deliberate edge approach practice.

Commitment Moment: What edge will you deliberately explore in the next seven days?

Edge domain:

Current capacity:

10 percent challenge:

Implementation date:

Support needed:

Remember: True strength often emerges not despite our limitations but because of how they teach us to move differently. As we move into chapter 5, we'll explore how to convert these insights into sustainable action—not by forcing our original vision but by adapting our approach while maintaining our core purpose.

FIVE

CONVERTING INTERNAL STRENGTH TO SUSTAINABLE ACTION

FROM SPACE TO MOVEMENT

Who This Chapter Is For

- Individuals ready to transform insight into action
- Professionals seeking to implement sustainable change
- Entrepreneurs looking to operationalize vision
- Anyone who has struggled with maintaining momentum

Key Transformational Outcomes

By the end of this chapter, you will be able to do the following:

- Understand the mechanics of converting potential into consistent action
- Develop systems for sustainable implementation
- Learn to create optimal space for meaningful movement
- Build frameworks for maintaining long-term momentum
- Master the balance between structure and flexibility

UNDERSTANDING MOVEMENT THROUGH SPACE

Have you ever tried to cook in a cluttered kitchen where every movement became a negotiation with chaos? Or found yourself on a packed dance floor where the desire to move met the reality of restriction? These everyday experiences mirror a profound truth I discovered through my journey with osteoarthritis: Where there is no pure space, there can be no pure movement.

Reflection Point

Where in your life do you feel most compressed or restricted?

How does this compression affect your ability to take meaningful action?

What areas of your life have adequate space for movement?

THE KEY-LOCK PRINCIPLE OF MOVEMENT

Just as a key needs the right space to turn smoothly in a lock, our lives require specific types of space to enable meaningful change. When we try to force movement without first creating proper space, we often meet the same resistance as when we are trying to fit the wrong key into a lock—frustration, limitation, and ultimately, failure.

This connection between space and movement addresses challenges many face when attempting sustainable change.

- **The launch-fizzle cycle:** Repeatedly starting ambitious initiatives without proper conditions for success.

- **The implementation gap:** Understanding concepts intellectually but failing to translate them into consistent action.

- **The optimization trap:** Endlessly researching "perfect" approaches rather than beginning with simple, imperfect action.

Key insight: Sustainable action doesn't come from force or willpower, but from creating the right conditions for natural movement.

THE INTERNAL-EXTERNAL CONNECTION

While my early awareness of space began with my father's absence, my understanding truly crystallized years later in my work with physical therapists trained in functional range systems and postural restoration methodologies. As these specialists enhanced my manual therapy training, my eyes were finally opened to the profound significance of space across all life pillars. I discovered how fascia—the intricate web of connective tissue surrounding every muscle fiber, organ, and cell —creates an essential architecture that either enables or restricts movement. Working with these practitioners helped me fully comprehend how every fiber in the body interconnects and is tied to our breath and the synovial spaces that enable all physical movement.

Working with clients, I observed a pattern that would reshape my understanding of change: A physically strong client struggled with basic movements despite impressive external capabilities. His fascial restrictions created invisible barriers that no amount of force could overcome. This revealed a universal truth: External actions, no matter how powerful, cannot create lasting transformation without internal alignment.

Key implementation assessment: The following exercise helps you identify disconnects between your internal state and external actions. Where alignment is low, focus on internal shifts before attempting to force external changes. This inside-out approach creates more sustainable movement than exclusively targeting your behaviors.

For each dimension, describe your current internal condition and external behaviors, then honestly evaluate their alignment on a scale of one to ten. Where alignment is low, focus on creating internal shifts before attempting to force external changes. Use this framework to identify which dimensions would benefit most from internal recalibration versus those ready for external action.

Internal-External Alignment Assessment
Map your current alignment using the following framework.

Life Dimension	Internal State	External Actions	Alignment Score (1–10)	Adjustment Needed
Physical				
Mental				
Emotional				
Spiritual				
Professional				
Relational				
Financial				
Purpose				

Understanding this connection between our internal states and external actions helps explain why many implementation efforts fail despite strong motivation or clear goals. When we create appropriate internal conditions first, external actions flow naturally rather than requiring constant force or willpower.

Consider a practical example from biomechanics: If your arm cannot fully raise above your head without compensation in your spine, collarbone, or shoulder blade, you lack the internal prerequisites for that movement. Adding external load through overhead presses when these internal capabilities aren't established creates the perfect conditions for injury. The body will find a way to perform the movement, but at the cost of stressing joints, tendons, and ligaments in ways they weren't designed to handle.

This principle extends to cardiovascular training as well. Many enthusiasts focus exclusively on high-intensity interval training (HIIT), seeking maximum external performance while neglecting the internal foundation. Research shows that excessive HIIT without adequate base conditioning can lead to cardiac remodeling and an enlarged heart—a compensation pattern at the organ level.

In contrast, consistent zone one cardio (lower-intensity aerobic work) establishes the prerequisites of enhanced mitochondrial density, capillary development, and cardiac efficiency. This internal development creates the conditions for optimal performance and longevity, whereas skipping these foundations for immediate external results often leads to diminished capacity over time.

Similarly, trying to force external changes in any life dimension without first creating the internal conditions to support them leads to compensation, strain, and ultimately, breakdown of the system.

Integration Questions

- Where do you feel most disconnected between your internal state and external actions?
- What internal shifts might enable more effective external movement?
- Where are you forcing external change without internal alignment?

CREATING SUSTAINABLE SPACE FOR ACTION

Just as your joints need the right amount of synovial fluid—not too much, not too little—each area of life requires properly maintained space. Let's explore how to create and maintain this space across a few different dimensions.

1. **Physical Space: The Foundation of Movement**

Our physical environments shape our capacity for action. As a fitness concierge in 2006, I discovered that sustainable physical changes at the individual level correlated to collective benefits at the corporate level. A hotel-specific fitness challenge turned into a companywide fitness challenge among all of the corporation's properties in New York City. We garnered the assistance of insurance and corporate wellness providers to provide assessments prior to the start of the challenge and at the end of the challenge. We did this with minimal digital tools.

As noted, our physical environments significantly impact our capacity for movement. This audit helps you evaluate how different spaces in your life either support or restrict your action potential. For each environment, assess its current movement support, identify specific restriction points, explore optimization opportunities, and design practical implementation strategies. Focus on making small, consistent adjustments rather than complete overhauls, allowing your spaces to gradually evolve to better support your authentic movement patterns. Remember that environmental changes often create ripple effects across all other dimensions of life.

Physical Space Optimization Framework
Environmental Movement Audit

Physical Environment	Current Movement Support (1–10)	Restriction Points	Optimization Opportunities	Implementation Strategy
Home				
Workspace				
Daily Commute				
Exercise Areas				
Rest and Restoration Spaces				

Space Creation Strategy

A. **Immediate Environment Adjustments**

- Remove three objects that consistently impede your movement or create visual clutter.
- Rearrange furniture to create clearer pathways through your most frequently used spaces.
- Add one element that specifically supports your current growth priority in this environment.

B. **Progressive Environment Transformation**

- Experiment with one significant spatial change each day for one week, noting which create the most positive impact.

- Implement a systematic approach to reorganizing your space based on your week-one findings.
- Create a long-term plan for evolving your environment as your needs and priorities shift.

C. Maintenance Protocol

- Spend thirty seconds at the end of each day returning your environment to its optimal state.
- Each week, assess which environmental elements are supporting and which are hindering your movement goals.
- Schedule a more comprehensive environmental review that coincides with your monthly pillar assessment.

2. Mental Space: Creating Room for Clarity

My transition from operations management to full-time acting and improv student and aspiring artist taught me that mental space, like physical space, requires both structure and flexibility. The principle of "Yes, and …" used in improv—where performers accept whatever their scene partner offers ("yes") and then build upon it ("and")—goes beyond a mere warm-up routine. This fundamental technique creates forward momentum by transforming potential limitations into creative opportunities rather than obstacles.

This approach mirrors how great innovators today (and throughout history) work within constraints to create remarkable breakthroughs. Instead of rejecting limitations with "no" or "but," they find ways to acknowledge reality while expanding possibilities. What happens when we apply this same principle to our own perceived restrictions? How might apparent limitations actually contain untapped movement potential if approached with the flexible mindset of "Yes, and …" rather than rigid resistance?

To translate this principle into practice, you need to systematically evaluate your mental landscape just as you would assess your physical space. The following framework helps you identify specific areas of mental compression and opportunity across different domains of your thinking. For each mental domain, assess the quality of your current space, note particular restriction points, explore potential expansion opportunities, and design practical implementation strategies. This structured assessment creates the foundation for a comprehensive system of mental clarity rather than isolated techniques or inspirational concepts.

Mental Clarity Creation System
Mental Environment Assessment

Mental Domain	Current Space (1–10)	Compression Points	Expansion Opportunities	Implementation Strategy
Focus Capacity				
Decision-Making				
Creative Thinking				
Learning Integration				
Strategic Reflection				

Mental Space Creation Protocol

A. **Input Management Framework**

- Track your information sources for three days, noting which create clarity and which create confusion.
- Remove or significantly limit the three inputs that most consistently drain your mental energy.
- Identify and prioritize three to five information sources that consistently enhance your thinking.
- Develop a specific method for converting information into applicable knowledge.

B. **Processing Optimization**

- Implement a two-minute practice to clear mental static before beginning important cognitive work.
- Create a reliable system for capturing thoughts and ideas before they disappear.
- Establish a consistent format and schedule for reflecting on key experiences.
- Design a process for connecting new insights to your existing knowledge base.

C. **Output Enhancement**

- Develop criteria for making different types of decisions rather than using the same approach for everything.

- Establish specific environmental or time-based cues that automatically trigger implementation.
- Create a structured approach for incorporating feedback into your thinking and actions.
- Implement a regular review cycle to identify and upgrade your mental patterns.

Daily Mental Space Maintenance

- **Morning mental preparation ritual (five to ten minutes):** Begin your day by defining your thinking priorities and clearing potential distractions.
- **Midday mental reset practice (two to five minutes):** Pause to release accumulated mental tension and recalibrate your focus.
- **Evening mental integration protocol (ten to fifteen minutes):** Review key insights from the day and prepare your mind for restorative rest.

3. **Emotional Space: Creating Room for Authentic Expression**

Working with clients through physical transformation revealed that emotional space is often the missing link in sustainable change. Just as tight fascia restricts our physical movement, emotional constriction limits our capacity for authentic action.

Consider the hotel front desk agent who hasn't experienced a vacation in years. They find themselves in a position similar to a manual therapist who hasn't received treatment themselves—gradually disconnected from the very experience they're meant to facilitate. Without experiencing the rejuvenation they help create for others, they lose touch with their role's purpose and value. Front desk staff who lose connection to the profound impact they can have on a guest's stay open the door to stagnation in their performance and satisfaction. This disconnect becomes even more critical in luxury properties where guests' expectations are extraordinarily high and a single interaction can significantly impact both guest satisfaction and property reputation. Their emotional capacity becomes compressed, limiting their ability to genuinely connect with guests.

This pattern appears across many domains of life. When we don't create adequate emotional space and time to process our feelings, express authentically, and receive genuine connection, our actions become mechanical rather than meaningful. The restriction doesn't just affect our emotional well-being; it cascades through our entire system, limiting our professional effectiveness, physical vitality, and sense of purpose.

Creating proper emotional space isn't a luxury but a necessity for sustainable performance and authentic presence in all areas of life. But emotional capacity, like physical strength, requires intentional development and maintenance. This assessment helps you evaluate how different emotional patterns affect your available space and identify specific opportunities for expansion. For each pattern, consider its current impact on your space, note particular constriction points, explore possible expansion opportunities, and design practical implementation strategies. The subsequent protocol provides structured approaches for developing awareness, implementing expansion strategies, and integrating new emotional capacities into your daily life—creating a sustainable system for emotional growth rather than sporadic attempts at change.

Emotional Space Creation Framework
Emotional Environment Assessment

Emotional Pattern	Space Impact (1–10)	Constriction Points	Expansion Opportunities	Implementation Strategy
Processing Emotions				
Emotional Range				
Vulnerability Capacity				
Emotional Resilience				
Authenticity Expression				

Emotional Space Creation Protocol

A. Awareness Development

- Develop a daily habit of naming your emotions without judgment, using a broad vocabulary beyond basic feelings like "good" or "bad."
- Track how your emotions manifest in your body (tension, energy, temperature) to recognize your feelings before they intensify.
- Document situations, interactions, and thoughts that consistently evoke strong emotional responses.

B. Expansion Strategy

- Create designated spaces and times for authentic emotional release, such as journaling, trusted conversations, or creative expression.
- Develop a tiered approach to sharing your feelings, starting with minor disclosures and gradually increasing depth with proven safe connections.
- Systematically increase your ability to sit with uncomfortable emotions through timed exposure, gradually extending your tolerance.

C. **Integration Framework**

- Implement brief regular pauses to assess your emotional state, perhaps tied to transitions in your day.
- Establish a dedicated time for deeper emotional exploration, integration, and release.
- Review emotional patterns, celebrate growth, and intentionally stretch your emotional comfort zone in controlled ways.

4. **Financial Space: Creating Room for Resource Flow**

Working in Wall Street during market upheavals taught me that financial space isn't just about money—it's about creating room for adaptation and growth. From a distance, I watched the post-pandemic contrast between IWG (Regus) and WeWork, and I noticed how sustainable space creation outperforms rapid expansion.

While both companies faced significant challenges during the pandemic, IWG's established business model, broader geographic diversification, and lower debt burden allowed it to weather the storm more effectively. WeWork, despite its innovative approach, struggled with the financial constraints of its prepandemic rapid expansion, ultimately leading to bankruptcy protection in late 2023. IWG's ability to maintain financial flexibility and adapt its offerings to changing work patterns enabled it to navigate past restrictions more effectively, highlighting how financial space creates resilience during market disruptions.

The following assessment helps you evaluate different financial domains, identifying specific restriction points and expansion opportunities. For each resource category, assess its current state, note limitation patterns, explore potential movement possibilities, and design practical implementation strategies. The subsequent protocol provides structured approaches for eliminating restrictions, optimizing flow, and expanding capacity—creating a comprehensive system for financial freedom rather than isolated budgeting or investment techniques.

Financial Movement Optimization System
Resource Flow Assessment

Financial Domain	Current Space (1–10)	Restriction Points	Expansion Opportunities	Implementation Strategy
Income Stream				
Expense Structure				
Savings Capacity				
Investment Movement				
Financial Flexibility				

Financial Space Creation Protocol

A. Restriction Identification

- Review and identify expenses that don't align with your values or priorities.
- Simplify complex financial systems that create mental clutter or confusion.
- Track where resources are leaking out without providing meaningful return.

B. Flow Optimization

- Develop multiple income sources to reduce dependency on any single stream.
- Create a clear framework for allocating resources based on your priorities.
- Implement strategies to improve timing of inflows and outflows for stability.

C. Capacity Expansion

- Establish financial buffer zones to absorb unexpected expenses.
- Develop a dedicated fund for pursuing new opportunities without strain.
- Build systems that increase your financial flexibility during periods of change.

Financial Mobility Framework

- **Daily financial awareness practice:** Take sixty seconds each day to notice one financial decision and consider its alignment with your values.

- **Weekly financial movement review:** Identify patterns in your resource flows and assess which money movements created the most value.
- **Monthly financial space assessment:** Evaluate how your financial boundaries and practices are supporting or restricting movement in other life dimensions.

IMPLEMENTATION STRATEGY: CREATING DAILY SPACE FOR ACTION

This chapter bridges theory and practice, providing concrete tools for translating your insights into consistent, sustainable action. The frameworks that follow create a progressive implementation system: Daily practices establish momentum, weekly boundaries maintain direction, and monthly integration ensures evolution. This multilayered approach addresses the common gap between understanding and application.

Just as maintaining joint health requires daily attention, creating sustainable action space demands consistent, intentional practice. Let me share how I conceptualized how to create space while managing more than 180 team members across twenty-one luxury properties in New York City. Break your full system needs down into controllable blocks.

Foundational practice: The following daily framework creates the essential rhythm for sustainable movement. Begin by implementing just one component of this system rather than attempting the entire framework at once. As each element becomes integrated into your natural flow, gradually add others. Consistency with a minimal approach produces better results than sporadic implementation of the complete system.

DAILY IMPLEMENTATION FRAMEWORK

Morning Space Creation Protocol (Fifteen to Twenty Minutes)

A. **Physical Readiness (Three to Five Minutes)**

- Conduct a brief body scan, noting areas of tension, and mobilize stiff joints.
- Activate your energy through breath work or gentle movement.
- Prepare your body for the day with targeted movement in areas that need attention.

B. **Mental Clarity (Five to Seven Minutes)**

- Capture racing thoughts by writing them down or speaking them aloud.
- Identify your one to three most important priorities for the day.
- Enhance focus by clearing distractions and creating a mental container for your work.

C. **Emotional Alignment (Three to Five Minutes)**

- Check in with your current emotional state without judgment.
- Intentionally generate emotions that will support your day's objectives.
- Visualize yourself moving through the day in an aligned and centered state.

D. **Day Architecture (Three to Five Minutes)**

- Schedule your day based on your core values rather than just urgency.
- Create buffer zones between activities to allow for transition and recovery.
- Plan specific recovery points throughout your day to maintain a sustainable energy level.

Personalized rhythm framework: The following structure helps you create an intentional flow throughout your day, identifying specific times for focused action, space creation, and recovery. Customize this framework to align with your natural energy patterns and external commitments rather than forcing an arbitrary schedule

Complete this table based on your natural energy patterns throughout the day. Identify specific times when you typically have high energy for focused work and when you need recovery periods.

Day Flow Management System

Time Block	Focus Purpose	Space Creation Strategy	Implementation Trigger	Recovery Protocol
Morning				
Midmorning				
Midday				
Afternoon				
Evening				

Evening Integration Practice (Ten to Fifteen Minutes)

A. **Day Review (Three to Five Minutes)**

- Reflect on where you created movement today and where you felt restricted.
- Evaluate how effectively you utilized space in each pillar.
- Note any recurring patterns in your movement or restriction.

B. **System Adjustment (Three to Five Minutes)**

- Identify one process that could be refined tomorrow.
- Determine where you could create more space for movement.
- Consider how to optimize your implementation approach.

C. **Next-Day Preparation (Three to Five Minutes)**

- Set one to three clear priorities aligned with your movement goals.
- Prepare your physical and mental environment for tomorrow.
- Establish a clear intention for how you want to move.

While daily practices create immediate movement, weekly structures ensure this movement maintains coherent direction. The following framework helps you establish the necessary boundaries for sustained progress while preventing scattered efforts.

WEEKLY BOUNDARIES AND ASSESSMENT: CREATING SUSTAINED MOMENTUM

Like a joint needs periods of recovery between loading sessions, our lives require clear boundaries for sustainable performance. Boundaries are like oil in an engine, allowing all the parts to work collectively. Mapping out your boundaries will enhance your assessment and action plan. This framework will also help you establish necessary boundaries for sustained progress while preventing scattered efforts; you'll create sustainable momentum rather than cycles of enthusiasm followed by depletion. Use the weekly review practice to evaluate progress across all pillars, identify emerging patterns, and make strategic adjustments that maintain alignment with your deeper purpose.

Weekly Sustainability Framework

Boundary Creation Protocol

A. **Energy Management System**

- Identify your highest-energy periods for next week and allocate your most important tasks to these times.
- Note any recovery needs based on this week's depletion patterns.
- Establish clear signals that will trigger boundary enforcement when needed.

B. **Space Maintenance Audit**

- Review how your physical environments supported or restricted your movement this week.
- Assess your mental clarity patterns and what influenced them.
- Check your emotional space. Where did you feel compressed, and where did you feel expansive?
- Evaluate how your environments could be optimized next week.

C. **System Adjustment Framework**

- Identify one process that needs refinement based on this week's experience.
- Adjust any boundaries that proved either too rigid or too permeable.
- Select one implementation area to enhance for the coming week.

Weekly Review Practice (Thirty to Sixty Minutes)

Review Area	Assessment Questions	Adjustment Strategy	Implementation Plan
Physical Movement			
Mental Clarity			
Emotional Space			
Spiritual Journey			
Professional Trajectory			
Relationship Dynamics			
Financial Flow			
Purpose Alignment			

MONTHLY EVOLUTION AND INTEGRATION: CREATING SUSTAINABLE GROWTH

Just as joint health requires regular reassessment and adjustment, our lives need monthly check-ins to ensure we're creating the right kind of space for growth. My own experience with intentional downsizing powerfully illustrates this principle.

After selling our two-bedroom house in Ozone Park, New York, my family and I made the conscious decision to transition to a one-bedroom apartment nearby. This wasn't merely downsizing—it was strategic restriction. We recognized that creating space in one dimension often generated unexpected possibilities in others.

The decision represented a fundamental principle of the Synovial Space approach: Sometimes, we must intentionally create restriction in one area to enable greater movement across our entire system. Despite having two children, we embraced this constraint by applying the 80/20 principle to our possessions—keeping only the 20 percent that created 80 percent of our value and joy. What initially seemed like a restriction became a catalyst for transformation.

This physical downsizing created unexpected space in other dimensions of our lives. With reduced financial obligations and simplified logistics, I found the freedom to step away from operations management and pursue acting training—a professional shift that would have seemed impossible in our previous lifestyle. The financial margin created by our smaller living arrangement allowed us to build reserves that eventually supported our cross-country relocation to California.

What this experience taught me was profound: Sometimes, creating literal space by removing physical objects opens up metaphorical space across multiple life pillars. Our monthly assessment practice helped us recognize these connection points and capitalize on the momentum they created.

Strategic integration point: The monthly review process represents a critical integration moment in your movement practice. Unlike daily or weekly check-ins, this deeper assessment helps you recognize subtle patterns, anticipate emerging challenges, and realign with your evolving purpose. Take time to deliberately celebrate even the smallest signs of progressive movement during these assessments, as acknowledging these microshifts reinforces the neural pathways that support continued growth. Consider integrating these reviews into your digital calendar system with automated reminders, or using simple note-taking applications to track patterns over time. The specific technology matters less than establishing a consistent system that works within your existing routines. Schedule this practice during a time when you can engage with genuine curiosity rather than evaluation pressure.

Monthly Evolution System

Comprehensive Assessment Protocol

A. **Movement Pattern Analysis**

- **Physical capacity evaluation:** Measure specific changes in your movement capabilities across primary joints and functional patterns.
- **Mental clarity assessment:** Evaluate how your thought patterns have evolved and where new mental space has emerged.
- **Emotional range review:** Document shifts in your emotional responses and identify areas of expanded expression.

B. **Financial Flow Analysis**

- **Environmental support check:** Examine how your physical spaces are either enhancing or restricting your movement potential.
- **Relationship dynamic mapping:** Identify how key relationships have evolved and where new connection patterns have emerged.
- **Purpose alignment gauge:** Assess how your daily activities align with your core values and longer-term vision.

C. **System Evolution Framework**

- **Pattern recognition method:** Look for recurring themes across all pillars that indicate systematic shifts.
- **Implementation refinement approach:** Adjust your practices based on what's creating the most significant movement.
- **Space optimization strategy:** Identify areas where creating more or less space would enhance overall system function.

D. **Growth Integration Protocol**

- **Expanded capacity integration:** Connect new capabilities in one pillar to potential movement in other pillars.
- **New pattern reinforcement:** Design specific practices to strengthen emerging positive patterns.
- **Evolution celebration practice:** Acknowledge and honor your growth to reinforce continued development.

Monthly Review Practice (One to Two Hours)

Evolution Domain	Progress Assessment	Pattern Recognition	Next-Level Strategy	Implementation Plan
Physical				
Mental				
Emotional				
Spiritual				
Professional				
Relational				
Financial				
Purpose				

The following tools translate the principles you've learned into practical applications. Each addresses a specific aspect of implementation, providing a structured approach to creating and maintaining space for movement. While you may be drawn to the tools that seem most relevant to your current challenges, experiment with each one to discover unexpected insights and possibilities.

Practical Implementation Tools

1. Space Creation Assessment Tool

Use this framework to reevaluate your current space across all dimensions and identify continued opportunities for optimization. Remember to focus on the connections between pillars rather than viewing them as isolated domains—often, creating space in one dimension naturally generates movement in others.

Comprehensive Space Assessment
Rate each domain on a scale of 1-10.
(1 = highly compressed, 10 = optimal space)

Life Dimension	Current Space Rating	Key Restriction Points	Space Creation Opportunity	Immediate Action Step
Physical				
Mental				
Emotional				
Spiritual				
Professional				
Relational				
Financial				
Purpose				

Daily maintenance practice: This structured approach ensures consistent attention to creating and maintaining space across all dimensions. Begin with just the morning or evening practice before implementing the full protocol.

2. Daily Space Creation Protocol

Implement this daily practice to maintain optimal space for movement across all dimensions.

Daily Space Maintenance System

Morning Space Creation (Five to Fifteen Minutes)

A. **Physical Space**

- **Body scan and tension release:** Take sixty seconds to identify and release tension in your three most common holding areas.
- **Movement preparation:** Perform mobility exercises for the joints you'll use most during your day.
- **Environment optimization:** Adjust your immediate surroundings to support your primary tasks.

B. **Mental Space**

- **Thought-capture exercise:** Write down any recurring thoughts to clear them from active processing.
- **Focus enhancement technique:** Define your three most important thinking tasks for the day.
- **Priority alignment:** Connect today's activities with your longer-term goals and values.

C. **Emotional Space**

- **Feeling identification practice:** Name your current emotional state without judgment.
- **Intentional state creation:** Generate the emotional quality that would best serve your day.
- **Expression opportunity:** Allow one genuine emotional expression before entering performance mode.

Midday Space Reset (Two to Five Minutes)

A. **Physical Reset**

- **Movement microbreak:** Change your physical position and move the joints that have been static.
- **Isometric pulses:** Generate light muscle tension in static positions to energize and increase blood flow.
- **Energy restoration:** Use a targeted breathing pattern to refresh your physical state.

B. **Mental Refresh**

- **Attention refocus practice:** Clear mental distractions and return to your priority tasks.
- **Priority reassessment:** Adjust your focus based on what's emerged since the morning.
- **Clarity enhancement:** Create mental space by stepping back from the details to see the bigger picture.

C. **Emotional Recalibration**

- **Emotional check-in:** Notice how your emotional state has shifted since the morning.
- **State adjustment:** Make one specific change to your emotional atmosphere as needed.
- **Authentic expression:** Share or acknowledge a genuine feeling rather than suppressing it.

Evening Integration (Five to Fifteen Minutes)

A. **Physical Integration**

- **Body relaxation practice:** Positively release accumulated tension from the day's activities.
- **Movement reflection:** Note how your body responded to the day's challenges.
- **Recovery preparation:** Set up your environment for optimal physical restoration.

B. **Mental Integration**

- **Thought-capture exercise:** Document insights and unresolved questions from the day.
- **Learning integration:** Identify one significant lesson to incorporate into your understanding.
- **Next-day preparation:** Clear mental space by defining tomorrow's priorities.

C. **Emotional Integration**

- **Feeling acknowledgment practice:** Honor the full range of emotions experienced today.
- **Expression completion:** Resolve any emotional experiences that feel unfinished.
- **Emotional reset:** Create the optimal emotional state for restoration and recovery.

Application in practice: The impact of these daily space creation practices can be profound, even when they are implemented in small ways. One client struggling with consistent physical movement found that her morning routine actually created compression rather than space. By implementing a five-minute breathing practice before checking her phone, she created internal space that naturally led to more consistent physical movement throughout her day. This small adjustment to her internal environment produced more significant results than her previous attempts to force external behavior changes.

Consistency framework: This system helps overcome the implementation gap by creating reliable cues for your space creation practices. Identifying multiple trigger types increases the likelihood of consistent practice.

3. Implementation Trigger System

Creating reliable triggers that automatically initiate your space creation practices is essential for consistent implementation. This framework helps you identify multiple cue types for each practice, increasing the likelihood of regular execution. For each space creation activity, determine specific location triggers, time signals, activity prompts, and sensory cues that will naturally remind you to implement the practice. This multilayered approach prevents reliance on willpower alone, creating environmental and behavioral triggers that make space creation increasingly automatic. Begin by establishing just two or three strong triggers for your most crucial practices before expanding to a more comprehensive system.

Implementation Trigger Framework

Practice	Location Trigger	Time Trigger	Activity Trigger	Sensory Trigger
Morning Space Creation				
Focus Enhancement				
Movement Integration				
Emotional Processing				
Boundary Maintenance				
Evening Integration				

These implementation tools were designed to be an integrated system: The assessment identifies where space is needed, the daily protocol creates consistent practice, and the trigger framework ensures reliable implementation. Together, they transform insights into embodied action while maintaining the essential space needed for sustainable movement.

As you continue working with these frameworks and completing these exercises, you'll likely experience an important shift in perspective that distinguishes the Synovial Space methodology from other life coaching approaches. Unlike traditional coaching models that often focus primarily on goal achievement or mindset shifts in isolation, this methodology creates a systematic exploration of the spaces between restriction and possibility across all life dimensions.

What initially appears as a simple assessment often becomes a doorway to unexpected insights. Many clients report that the mere act of mapping their current space across a few different dimensions reveals movement possibilities they hadn't previously considered. This is by design—the structured nature of these exercises doesn't just document your current state but also creates the conditions for new awareness. The questions themselves become tools that open space for movement, demonstrating how our perception of restriction often conceals hidden pathways forward.

Where conventional approaches might have you pushing against limitations or attempting to overcome them through force of will, the Synovial Space methodology invites you to work with restrictions, finding the precise amount of space needed for optimal movement—not too little, not too much. This balance point, like the synovial fluid in a healthy joint, creates the conditions for sustainable action rather than dramatic but unsustainable change.

INTEGRATION: THE SPACE-ACTION CONNECTION

Just as healthy joints create the foundation for fluid physical movement, properly maintained space across all life dimensions creates the foundation for sustainable action. By systematically creating and maintaining these spaces, you establish the conditions for natural, effortless movement.

Recall the perspective shift that astronauts experience when viewing Earth from space—how the artificial boundaries we create dissolve into a single, interconnected system. When you properly integrate these implementation frameworks, a similar shift occurs within your life. The separate pillars merge into a unified architecture where movement flows naturally between dimensions. Just as returning astronauts bring their expanded perspective back to everyday challenges, you'll approach daily actions with a newfound awareness of how each small movement contributes to your entire system's evolution. This integration transforms isolated practices into a coherent ecosystem where actions arise not from forced effort but from aligned intention.

The integration of these implementation frameworks creates a sustainable architecture for ongoing movement. Rather than relying solely on motivation or willpower, this system establishes the conditions where movement emerges naturally. As you implement these practices, you'll discover that consistent, small actions create more significant and lasting change than sporadic, dramatic efforts.

DEVELOPING PRESENT AWARENESS THROUGH PRACTICE

As you consistently implement these daily maintenance practices, something remarkable will begin to emerge beyond the immediate benefits in each pillar. You'll develop what might be called a restriction awareness system—an increasingly sensitive internal gauge that spontaneously signals when a pillar falls too far out of alignment.

This awareness isn't something you need to consciously cultivate; rather, it emerges naturally from the practice itself. The consistent attention to space across all dimensions gradually attunes your system to recognize restriction before it becomes problematic. Like a well-calibrated joint that instinctively knows its optimal range, your integrated awareness begins to signal when adjustment is needed.

This phenomenon creates a feedback loop where your growing sensitivity to imbalance allows for earlier, more subtle interventions. What begins as deliberate practice evolves into intuitive knowing. The very act of seeking movement past restrictions becomes a practice of presence—anchoring you in the now while simultaneously expanding your capacity for the future.

This is perhaps the most powerful aspect of the Synovial Space methodology: Beyond the specific benefits in each pillar, it develops your capacity to inhabit the present moment with heightened awareness, creating a natural regulation system that maintains optimal space across your entire life architecture.

Key Chapter Takeaways

1. Sustainable action requires proper space creation.
2. Each life dimension needs a specific type of space.
3. Daily maintenance creates long-term sustainability.
4. Implementation requires both structure and flexibility.
5. Space creation is an ongoing practice, not a one-time event.

Your Immediate Next Steps

1. Complete the Comprehensive Space Assessment.
2. Identify your most compressed life dimension.
3. Implement the Daily Space Creation Protocol.
4. Develop your Implementation Trigger System.
5. Schedule your first weekly boundary review.

Commitment moment: What one space creation practice will you implement within the next twenty-four hours?

Practice:

Implementation time:

Trigger:

Expected benefit:

Remember: Like maintaining optimal joint space, creating life space is an ongoing practice. Start with one tool, build consistency, and progressively add more as you develop capacity. The goal isn't perfection—it's creating sustainable space for movement and growth.

SIX
RECOVERY AND REST

THE ART OF REST

Who This Chapter Is For

- Individuals experiencing burnout or diminishing returns
- Professionals struggling with sustainable performance
- Leaders seeking to build resilience in themselves and in their teams
- Anyone caught in a cycle of overexertion and collapse

Key Transformational Outcomes

By the end of this chapter, you will be able to do the following:

- Understand the critical role of recovery in sustainable performance
- Recognize the warning signs of recovery deficit
- Develop personalized restoration strategies for each life dimension
- Create systems for proactive rather than reactive recovery
- Build a comprehensive resilience framework for long-term sustainability

This chapter explores the often-overlooked cornerstone of sustainable movement: strategic recovery. Far from being an optional luxury, recovery is the essential counterpart to growth, creating the conditions where transformation becomes sustainable rather than depleting. The frameworks that follow will help you design personalized recovery systems that enhance rather than diminish your capacity for meaningful action.

UNDERSTANDING PAIN AND PROGRESS: THE RECOVERY PARADOX

Sometimes, recovery itself requires recovery. Like the synovial space in our joints needs maintenance to function optimally, our capacity for healing demands its own kind of space. This truth revealed itself to me through my ongoing journey with chronic pain.

Reflection Point

When have you pushed through fatigue only to diminish your results?

How do you currently distinguish between productive discomfort and harmful strain?

What signals does your body and mind send when recovery is needed?

THE PAIN CUP: UNDERSTANDING CAPACITY LIMITS

Imagine your brain as a cup that's constantly being filled with pain signals. The varying aches at any given moment create a persistent burden, a tightening sensation within your skull from the overload of painful synapses. This constant pain can gut-punch even the strongest will and sour the brightest day.

The pain cup isn't just a metaphor—it represents a neurological reality where our brain's capacity to process signals has actual limits. When this capacity becomes overwhelmed, all facets of performance decline regardless of motivation or discipline. Understanding and respecting these limits isn't weakness—it's the foundation of sustainable growth.

This pain cup concept mirrors common overload patterns many experience beyond physical pain.

- **Decision fatigue:** The cumulative weight of choices depletes mental resources.
- **Emotional saturation:** Constant exposure to others' needs fills one's capacity for empathy.
- **Attention fragmentation:** Endless notifications prevent deep concentration.

Key insight: Recovery is not a sign of weakness but a strategic necessity for sustainable performance.

THE CAPACITY ASSESSMENT FRAMEWORK

Just as understanding that joint capacity is essential for physical healing, recognizing your personal capacity limits is crucial for sustainable performance across all life dimensions. This assessment helps you evaluate your current resources in each pillar, identify specific warning signs of depletion, recognize unique restoration needs, and design personalized recovery strategies. Approach this framework with complete honesty, acknowledging both your strengths and limitations without judgment. This assessment creates the essential starting point for strategic recovery planning—identifying which areas most need restoration and which approaches might prove most effective.

Comprehensive Capacity Assessment
Rate your current capacity in each dimension (1–10).
(1 = completely depleted, 10 = optimally resourced)

Life Dimension	Current Capacity	Warning Signs	Restoration Needs	Recovery Strategy
Physical				
Mental				
Emotional				
Spiritual				
Professional				
Relational				
Financial				
Purpose				

Coaching Moment: Pain Patterns

Consider your own relationship with pain and recovery.

- What fills your daily pain cup?
- How do you typically respond to overload?
- Where might you need new recovery strategies?

FINDING STRENGTH IN CONTEXT: THE PERSPECTIVE PRINCIPLE

Just forty miles from where I write this book, aspiring Navy SEAL candidates endure the freezing Pacific Ocean. Always wet, always sandy, facing challenges that would be unimaginable to most. This knowledge provides perspective—there are always others willing to "embrace the suck" for something bigger than themselves.

But here's the crucial lesson: Even the strongest warrior sometimes needs to ring the bell. And in that moment, the one doing the ringing must find a new path forward.

Perspective Reframing Tool

When facing recovery resistance, use this reframing exercise.

1. Current challenge:

2. Perspective scale (1–10):

   (1 = minor inconvenience, 10 = maximum human suffering)
   Rate your initial perception of this challenge's severity, noting your immediate emotional response.

3. **Reference Points**

   - **Historical parallel:** Identify a historical figure who faced similar or greater challenges, and assess how they responded to create context for your situation.
   - **Contemporary comparison:** Consider someone in today's world who is facing a similar or more intense version of your challenge, noting their circumstances.
   - **Previous personal challenge:** Recall a time when you successfully navigated a comparable or more difficult situation, and review what strategies worked.

4. **Recalibrated Perspective**

   - **Rightful attention:** Based on your reference points, determine what level of attention this challenge genuinely warrants in your life.
   - **Appropriate recovery:** Define specific recovery practices that match the recalibrated importance of this challenge.
   - **Strategic response:** Create a concrete action plan with a time frame and the resources needed to address this challenge without overresponding or underresponding.

I've found that while perspective helped me contextualize my challenges, gaining perspective alone didn't eliminate my need for actual recovery strategies during my most difficult periods. When I was managing chronic pain while balancing demanding professional roles, just thinking differently about my situation wasn't enough—I needed concrete recovery practices. The frameworks that follow come from years of discovering how strategic rest and restoration actually enhance performance rather than diminish it, contradicting the "no pain, no gain" mindset that nearly broke me early in my journey.

THE RECOVERY PARADOX: BEYOND "NO PAIN, NO GAIN"

The fitness industry's mantra of "no pain, no gain" creates a dangerous narrative about progress. Like many, I initially resisted strategic recovery. Though my military dreams had been derailed by physical limitations before they'd ever started, I continued pushing myself to extremes in other areas.

This resistance to recovery reflects challenges many face with rest and restoration.

- **Productivity addiction:** Self-worth becomes tied to constant output.
- **Scarcity thinking:** Time appears too limited for recovery.
- **Social comparison:** Rest seems like a luxury while peers appear to maintain relentless paces.

High performers across various domains approach recovery differently, from minimalists like Elon Musk to athletes who prioritize extensive restoration protocols. This assessment helps you identify your personal resistance patterns that might prevent optimal functioning according to your unique needs. For each recovery barrier you recognize, explore its origin, evaluate its impact on your performance and well-being, develop an approach that better serves your specific goals, and design practical implementation strategies. This honest examination transforms recovery from an abstract concept into a personalized practice, addressing the underlying beliefs that may limit your sustainability despite your best intentions.

Recovery Resistance Assessment
Identify your recovery barriers.

Recovery Resistance	Origin	Impact (1–10)	Alternative Belief	Implementation Strategy
"Rest is weakness."				
"I don't have time."				
"Others don't rest."				
"I'll fall behind."				
"Recovery is lazy."				

Common Recovery Myths versus Reality

Recovery Myth	Scientific Reality	Personal Application
"Rest equals weakness."	"Growth happens during recovery."	
"Recovery is only for injury."	"Strategic rest enhances performance."	
"More effort always equals better results."	"Sustainable progress requires integration."	
"Breaks reduce productivity."	"Recovery is active, not passive."	

TYPES OF RECOVERY: UNDERSTANDING THE STRATEGIC RESTORATION SPECTRUM

Just as our synovial spaces need different types of maintenance, recovery takes various forms. Through my experience applying movement studies to my osteoarthritis and ossification condition, I've learned to distinguish between different recovery strategies.

The following framework distinguishes between these different types of recovery strategies—both active and passive. This distinction is crucial for effective implementation, as different depletion patterns require different restoration approaches.

For active recovery strategies like movement-based, cognitive, emotional, relational, and creative approaches, identify which best address your specific depletion patterns. Similarly, for passive strategies including physical rest, mental stillness, emotional space, environmental simplification, and digital detox, determine which create the most significant restoration for your system.

Understanding these varied strategies helps you design recovery protocols tailored to your specific needs rather than relying on generic approaches. I've provided examples in each passive and active category to illustrate the framework, but I encourage you to replace or supplement these with your own recovery strategies that resonate with your unique circumstances and preferences.

Recovery Typology Framework
Active Recovery Strategies

Recovery Type	Examples	Appropriate When ...	Implementation Method	Effectiveness Measure
Movement-Based	Gentle yoga, walking in nature, swimming, tai chi, controlled articular rotations	After prolonged sitting, mental fatigue, or emotional stress, or when feeling physically stagnant	15–30 minutes of intentional movement at 40–60% effort, focusing on breath and body awareness	Increased range of motion, mental clarity, reduced tension, improved energy
Cognitive	Reading fiction, strategic games, puzzles, learning a new skill, guided meditation	Following intense analytical work, decision fatigue, or information overload	Engage with material using different mental pathways, with clear time boundaries	Renewed focus, creative insights, decreased mental fog, improved problem-solving
Emotional	Journaling, trusted conversations, expressive arts, mindfulness	After emotionally charged events, during high stress, or when feeling numb	Create safe space for authentic expression with containment boundaries	Emotional clarity, reduced emotional intensity, increased range, sense of resolution
Relational	Quality time, meaningful conversations, collaborative projects	Following isolation, after difficult interactions, during transitions	Schedule intentional connection with purpose and boundaries	Decreased isolation, renewed perspective, sense of belonging, buoyancy
Creative	Free writing, unstructured drawing, improvisation, music, unplanned cooking	When stuck in rigid patterns or low inspiration, during implementation fatigue	Process-focused expression with minimal judgment, no outcome expectations	New insights, enthusiasm, novel connections, renewed possibility

While active recovery strategies engage energy systems in restorative ways, passive approaches create space for complete system rest. Both have important roles in a comprehensive recovery strategy, with their effectiveness depending on your specific depletion patterns and needs.

Passive Recovery Strategies

Recovery Type	Examples	Appropriate When ...	Implementation Method	Effectiveness Measure
Physical Rest	Restorative sleep, sauna sessions, massage therapy, floating tanks, low-intensity stretching practice	After intense physical exertion, during illness/injury, when experiencing physical fatigue or persistent tension	Create an optimal sleep environment, schedule regular bodywork, implement complete nonmovement periods	Decreased physical tension, improved sleep quality, reduced pain levels, natural energy return
Mental Stillness	Meditation, sensory deprivation, silent retreats, intentional boredom periods, gazing practices	During information overload, after prolonged focus/concentration, when experiencing racing thoughts or decision fatigue	Designate specific times for nonthinking, create a distraction-free environment, use guided approaches initially if needed	Reduced mental chatter, improved focus when returning to tasks, decreased anxiety, clearer priorities
Emotional Space	Boundaries from emotional triggers, permission for emotional neutrality, solitude, receiving rather than giving support	After emotionally intense experiences, during grief/processing, when experiencing compassion fatigue or emotional overwhelm	Create temporal or physical distance from emotional demands, communicate clear boundaries, use containment practices	Renewed emotional capacity, increased patience, return of empathy, reduced emotional reactivity
Digital Detox	Tech-free periods, notification sabbaticals, screen-free activities, analog alternatives, digital simplification	After prolonged screen use, during attention fragmentation, when experiencing digital anxiety or comparison effects	Set clear tech boundaries (time/space/app-specific), remove devices from certain areas, use blocking tools if needed	Improved attention span, decreased fear of missing out (FOMO), enhanced face-to-face connections, more embodied presence

Coaching Moment: Recovery Assessment

Consider your current recovery patterns.

- Which type of recovery do you typically choose?
- Where might you need more active recovery?
- When is passive recovery more appropriate?
- What new recovery approaches might benefit you most?

THE JOINT-CENTERED APPROACH: LESSONS FROM FUNCTIONAL RANGE SYSTEMS

Traditional fitness approaches often focus on linear movements that build surface-level strength while neglecting the actual joint health that enables sustainable movement. This creates an illusion of progress—in terms of visible muscle development and performance gains—while potentially accelerating joint degradation beneath the surface. What appears as growth may actually diminish long-term capacity.

According to functional range systems, developed by Dr. Andreo Spina, a fundamental truth about human physiology is recognized: Entropy—the tendency of systems to move toward disorder— affects our joints just as it affects all aspects of life. Without intentional, consistent countermeasures, our range of motion diminishes, tissues lose elasticity, and movement patterns become restricted.

This principle extends beyond physical function to all eight pillars. Just as controlled articular rotations combat physical entropy, our deliberate recovery practices counteract the natural degradation that occurs in every life dimension when left unattended.

The evidence is compelling: Studies show that up to 80 percent of professional athletes develop osteoarthritis or significant joint degeneration by middle age, often experiencing these issues decades earlier than the general population. Despite their apparent physical prowess, many former athletes struggle with chronic inflammation, compromised immune function, and systemic deterioration—the hidden costs of prioritizing external achievement over internal sustainability.

This pattern perfectly mirrors what happens in our broader lives when we focus exclusively on external achievements while neglecting our internal systems. Just as functional range conditioning (FRC) prioritizes controlled articular rotations that strengthen the actual joint structures rather than just surrounding muscles, true sustainable growth requires attention to the spaces that enable movement—not just the movement itself.

Consider how many high-performing individuals appear successful by external metrics while experiencing progressive internal depletion. Like the bodybuilder with impressive musculature but deteriorating joint function, they exhibit the markers of success while their fundamental capacity for movement diminishes.

The recovery paradox emerges from this understanding: Just as controlled articular rotations create stronger joints than conventional strength training alone, strategic recovery practices build greater capacity than continuous output. This isn't merely a metaphor—it's the same principle operating at different scales of human functioning.

These resistance patterns don't just exist as abstract concepts—they manifest in concrete experiences that demonstrate the high cost of ignoring recovery needs. My own journey with this resistance revealed its consequences in particularly memorable ways.

THE COST OF IGNORING RECOVERY: A BIRTHDAY LESSON

Sometimes, the most powerful lessons about recovery come through painful experiences. During my time managing staffing across New York City properties, I learned this truth the hard way.

Picture this: It was my thirty-ninth birthday, and I had dinner plans at a steakhouse in Little Italy with a childhood friend. My schedule that day had me traversing Manhattan, Queens, and Brooklyn via subway, bus, and ferry in a suit and while carrying heavy training materials for staff, moving between meetings without breaks for food or water. By dinnertime, exhausted and dehydrated, I faced the excruciating pain of kidney stones—a condition that was exacerbated by the very birthday meal I'd been anticipating.

The Recovery Paradox Revealed

The sum collective of our life experience teaches us crucial lessons about recovery.

- When we don't create space for recovery intentionally, our bodies force it upon us.
- Recovery isn't just about rest—it's about creating sustainable systems.
- Prevention requires less space than emergency recovery.

Personal Recovery Failure Analysis

A. **Identify a Recent Recovery Failure**

Describe a specific situation when you needed recovery but didn't implement it effectively. Note when it occurred and what was happening in your life at that time.

B. **Warning Signs That Were Present**

- **Physical signals:** Note bodily sensations that indicated depletion, such as unusual fatigue, tension patterns, sleep disruptions, or changes in appetite.
- **Mental indicators:** Identify cognitive symptoms like difficulty focusing, decision fatigue, memory issues, or repetitive thought patterns.
- **Emotional markers:** Document feelings that signaled recovery needs, such as irritability, emotional numbness, disproportionate reactions, or decreased empathy.
- **Environmental cues:** Recognize external indicators like workspace disorganization, relationship tension, or reduced effectiveness in routine tasks.

C. **Resistance Points That Prevented Recovery**

- **Internal barriers:** Identify personal beliefs, thoughts, or habits that made you postpone recovery, such as perfectionistic standards or difficulty setting boundaries.
- **External pressures:** Document specific demands from work, relationships, or commitments that competed with your recovery needs.
- **Systematic issues:** Recognize larger patterns in your life structure that consistently undermine your recovery efforts, like role overload or inadequate support systems.

D. **Consequences of Delayed Recovery**

- **Immediate impacts:** List the direct effects you experienced within hours or days, such as decreased performance, relationship friction, or physical symptoms.
- **Medium-term effects:** Identify how this affected you over weeks following the recovery failure, including compounding stressors or compensatory behaviors.

- **Long-term costs:** Consider the extended impacts if this pattern had continued, including potential effects on your health, relationships, and goal achievement.

- **Prevention Strategy for the Future**
- **Early warning recognition:** Develop a specific plan to notice your unique depletion signals earlier, including regular check-in practices.
- **Resistance management:** Create strategies to address your identified barriers, such as prepared responses to common pressures.
- **Proactive recovery protocol:** Design a concrete, predetermined recovery approach that can be implemented at the first sign of depletion.

BUILDING SUSTAINABLE RECOVERY SYSTEMS: COMPREHENSIVE RESILIENCE FRAMEWORK

Creating sustainable recovery isn't just about knowing recovery strategies—it's about implementing them systematically. The following frameworks help you move from understanding recovery principles to embodying them in your daily practice, establishing the rhythms that create lasting resilience. Just as maintaining healthy synovial space requires consistent attention, sustainable recovery needs a systematic approach. The following frameworks provide practical tools for implementing strategic recovery across all dimensions.

1. Daily Recovery Assessment Tool

This daily check-in helps you identify subtle depletion signals before they escalate into system-wide fatigue. Consistently implementing this practice allows you to make small recovery adjustments that prevent the need for major resets, creating more sustainable energy management.

Passive Recovery Strategy
Daily Recover Check-In—Morning Assessment

Domain	Rating (1–10)	Warning Signs	Recovery Needed	Implementation Plan
Energy Level				
Mental Clarity				
Emotional Balance				
Physical Tension				
Motivation				

Recovery Signals Inventory
Track your personal warning signs.

Signal Category	Warning Signs	Intensity Threshold	Required Response
Physical Signals			
Mental Signals			
Emotional Signals			
Behavioral Signals			
Relational Signals			

2. Strategic Recovery Protocol

The following protocol translates recovery awareness into consistent practice. Rather than relying on sporadic or reactive approaches, this system creates reliable recovery rhythms throughout your day, preventing depletion before it occurs while enabling sustainable performance.

Implementation note: As a reminder, this comprehensive framework isn't meant to be adopted all at once. Begin by identifying your most significant recovery deficit based on your previous assessments—whether it's physical tension, mental fatigue, or emotional depletion. Then implement just one component of the morning reset protocol that directly addresses this primary need. After establishing this single practice consistently for two or three weeks, you might add another element or move to the midday reset component. Remember that incomplete implementation done consistently creates far greater benefits than perfect implementation attempted sporadically. The goal isn't to follow every suggestion but to develop a personalized recovery rhythm that works with your unique patterns and circumstances.

COMPREHENSIVE RECOVERY FRAMEWORK

Morning Reset Protocol

A. **Body Scan Practice**

- **Notice areas of tension:** Sequentially check each major joint and muscle group, noting specific locations of restriction or discomfort.
- **Assess energy levels:** Rate your current physical, mental, and emotional energy on a scale of one to ten, noting which systems need attention today.

- **Set recovery intentions:** Identify which pillar needs the most restoration focus in the next twenty-four hours.

B. **Implementation Method**

- **Morning ritual timing:** Determine the optimal five- to ten-minute window that can be consistently protected in your morning routine.
- **Key practices:** Select two or three specific reset activities that address your most common morning restrictions.
- **Environmental supports:** Prepare your physical space to minimize friction for completing your morning reset.

Midday Recovery Points

A. **Brief Restoration Practices**

- **Five-minute breathing resets:** Design a specific breathing pattern that counteracts your typical midday stress response.
- **Strategic movement breaks:** Identify movements that address the specific compensations created by your daily activities.
- **System check-in:** Create a quick assessment that scans all eight pillars to identify emerging depletion patterns.

B. **Implementation Triggers**

- **Time-based cues:** Schedule specific recovery moments that align with your natural energy fluctuations.
- **Environmental triggers:** Link recovery practices to existing environmental cues like entering specific spaces.
- **Warning sign responses:** Create immediate recovery protocols for your three most common depletion indicators.

Evening Integration

A. **Day Closure Practices**

- **Tension release ritual:** Develop a specific sequence that addresses the unique tension patterns created by your day.
- **Next-day preparation:** Create physical and mental space for tomorrow's priorities while maintaining boundaries.

- **Recovery needs assessment:** Identify which specific recovery practices would best prepare you for tomorrow's challenges.

B. **Implementation Method**

- **Evening routine timing:** Determine when your evening recovery window begins, and protect this transition point.
- **Key practices:** Select two or three consistent evening rituals that signal completion and prepare for restoration.
- **Environmental supports:** Design specific environmental adjustments that enhance your body's natural recovery processes.

3. Creating Recovery Boundaries: The Protection Framework

Just as a joint needs proper space to function, recovery requires clear boundaries. Through managing chronic pain, I've learned that boundaries aren't limitations—they're protection for sustainable performance. This framework helps you establish essential protection for your restoration practices across multiple domains. For time boundaries, you'll identify nonnegotiable rest periods, work/life separation strategies, digital detox windows, and dedicated recovery blocks. For energy boundaries, you'll develop assessment frameworks, task-scheduling approaches, commitment limitation strategies, and resource allocation methods. These structured protections don't restrict your freedom but rather create the necessary conditions for sustainable performance and authentic expression.

BOUNDARY DEVELOPMENT SYSTEM

Essential Recovery Boundaries

A. **Time Boundaries**

- **Nonnegotiable rest periods:** Identify specific blocks of time each day and week that are protected for restoration, regardless of external demands.
- **Work/life separation strategy:** Create concrete transition rituals between work and personal modes to prevent mental carryover.
- **Digital detox windows:** Designate specific hours when screens and notifications are completely eliminated.
- **Recovery blocks:** Schedule dedicated recovery activities with the same priority as your most important meetings.

B. **Energy Boundaries**

- **Priority assessment framework:** Develop a simple system to evaluate requests against your current capacity and core values.
- **Task scheduling approach:** Group similar activities to minimize context-switching costs and match tasks to natural energy rhythms.
- **Commitment limitation strategy:** Establish a maximum number of significant commitments you'll accept in any given period.
- **Energy allocation method:** Create a deliberate plan for distributing your resources across different life pillars each week.

BOUNDARY COMMUNICATION FRAMEWORK

The ability to clearly articulate and maintain boundaries is essential for sustainable movement across all eight pillars. Often, it's not the boundaries themselves but our communication approaches that determine whether they're respected.

The following framework provides practical language templates for common boundary scenarios, approaches to managing resistance, and strategies for consistent reinforcement. These templates are designed to be both professional and relationship-preserving—allowing you to protect your necessary space while maintaining effective connections.

Review these examples, then adapt the language and approach to align with your personal style and specific context. The goal isn't rigid adherence to these exact phrases but rather developing a consistent, clear approach to boundary communication that supports your overall movement capacity.

Boundary Communication Templates

Boundary Type	Communication Template	Resistance Management	Reinforcement Strategy
Time	"I've committed to being fully present with my family between 6 and 8 p.m. each evening. I'll be able to address this tomorrow morning at 9 a.m."	"I understand this feels urgent. Could you share what specific aspects need immediate attention so I can determine if this requires an exception to my family-time boundary?"	Set an automatic email response during boundary periods, turn off notifications, proactively inform colleagues of your time boundaries at the start of projects
Energy	"I'm at my capacity for new projects this month. I can review this again on [specific date] or help connect you with alternative resources now."	"I appreciate your confidence in me. Taking this on right now would compromise the quality of my existing commitments. Would you prefer to wait until [date] or explore alternatives?"	Track your energy expenditure like a budget, create a visual reminder of your current capacity, regularly reassess and communicate capacity updates
Digital	"I check emails/messages at 9 a.m., 1 p.m., and 4 p.m. daily. For urgent matters, please call my direct line."	"My structured communication schedule actually helps me respond more effectively to important requests. What's the timeline you're working with so I can plan accordingly?"	Use autoresponders explaining your system, batch communications during designated times, create clear criteria for what would be considered urgent
Availability	"I have thirty minutes available on Thursday at 2 p.m. or Friday at 11 a.m. Which works better for you?" (Versus "When are you free?")	"My calendar system helps ensure I'm fully present for each commitment. I can offer these specific times, or if none work, we can look at next week."	Use a scheduling system that only shows available times, preblock recovery and focus periods, confirm meeting purposes and durations in advance

Boundary Type	Communication Template	Resistance Management	Reinforcement Strategy
Commitment	"After reviewing my current projects and capacity, I can commit to [specific, limited version] rather than the full request."	"I want to deliver on everything I promise. Based on my current capacity, here's what I can realistically commit to with excellence …"	Document commitments explicitly, review requests against written criteria before accepting, schedule regular commitment inventory reviews

Examine Your Current Boundaries

- Where do you need stronger recovery boundaries?
- What makes maintaining boundaries difficult?
- How could better boundaries support your growth?
- What one boundary would create the most significant positive impact?

4. Emergency Recovery Protocols: Know When to Reset

Sometimes, despite our best planning, systems get overwhelmed. When life overwhelms your care-fully planned recovery system (and it will), having emergency protocols ready can prevent minor setbacks from becoming major crashes. I've found that preparation in four key areas makes all the difference: First, develop a few quick reset practices, like a specific breathing pattern that interrupts your stress response, a thought-stopping ritual you can use anywhere, and a grounding technique for emotional intensity. Second, identify your support system before you need it—know exactly who to call and what to say when you're depleted (I keep three people on my emergency contact list, each offering different kinds of support). Third, prepare boundary reinforcements—have ready responses for the inevitable demands that will arise during your recovery periods. Finally, know how you'll adjust your schedule when necessary, including which commitments can be rescheduled and how you'll communicate those changes respectfully. When my kidney stones struck during that birthday dinner in Little Italy, I had no emergency protocols in place—the recovery cost me weeks rather than days. Don't make my mistake.

SUSTAINABLE GROWTH THROUGH RECOVERY: PROGRESSIVE DEVELOPMENT FRAMEWORK

Understanding recovery is one thing—maintaining it is another. Just as I've learned to manage chronic pain through sustainable systems rather than quick fixes, long-term recovery, if feasible given your condition, requires both structure and adaptability. This framework helps you build sustainable restoration habits through systematic foundation building, ongoing monitoring of changing needs, and strategic adaptation over time.

Rather than attempting to implement advanced recovery practices immediately, begin with basic techniques that feel almost too easy, gradually increasing complexity and depth as your capacity expands. This progressive approach creates sustainable habits rather than temporary enthusiasm followed by abandonment.

Integration Practice

Create your personalized recovery system.

  A. **Choose One or Two Key Practices to Start**

- **Practice One:** Select one recovery technique that addresses your most immediate or significant depletion pattern.
- **Practice Two:** Identify a complementary practice that supports a different aspect of your system.

B. **Implementation Plan**

- **When:** Determine specific times that align with your natural rhythms and existing routines.
- **Where:** Designate physical locations that support these practices and minimize friction.
- **How long:** Establish realistic time frames that ensure consistency rather than occasional perfection.
- **Support needed:** Identify specific resources, people, or environments that will facilitate your success.

C. **Effectiveness Measurement**

- **Success indicators:** Define clear, observable markers that will demonstrate your recovery practices are working.
- **Adjustment criteria:** Establish specific conditions that would signal the need to modify your approach.

As you read these examples, identify at least one specific element from each case study that applies to your situation. Note how you might adapt their recovery approaches to your unique circumstances.

RECOVERY CASE STUDIES: REAL-WORLD IMPLEMENTATION

Case Study One: Executive Recovery Protocol

A CEO client of mine was experiencing declining performance despite working longer hours. Through implementing a strategic recovery protocol, she discovered that twenty minutes of midday restorative practice significantly improved her effectiveness. After six weeks of consistent practice, she reported completing high-priority tasks approximately 30 percent faster, making clearer decisions with fewer revisions, and experiencing noticeably more positive team interactions. Her executive assistant noted that meetings ran more efficiently, and team members commented on her improved listening skills and presence. While individual results will vary, this case illustrates how strategic recovery can enhance performance more effectively than extended work hours.

The following framework helps you calculate the return on your recovery investment—transforming the perception of recovery from "lost time" to "high-value investment." By honestly assessing current performance costs across productivity, decision quality, relationship impacts, and innovation limitations, you'll recognize the true price of insufficient restoration. Then, by calculating your time investment in recovery practices and projecting realistic returns, you'll develop a clearer understanding of recovery's actual value. This perspective shift often creates more consistent implementation by highlighting the concrete benefits rather than just the abstract importance.

Recovery ROI Calculator

Calculate your potential recovery return on investment.

A. **Current Performance Costs**

- **Productivity reduction (percentage):** Estimate how much your output decreases when operating without adequate recovery.
- **Decision quality impact (percentage):** Assess how your judgment and choices are affected by insufficient restoration.
- **Relationship strain (percentage):** Evaluate how your connections suffer when you're operating from depletion.
- **Innovation limitation (percentage):** Consider how your creativity and problem-solving capacity are constrained when underrecovered.

B. **Recovery Investment**

- **Daily time investment (minutes):** Calculate the total minutes dedicated to intentional recovery practices each day.
- **Weekly practices (time):** Quantify the additional time spent on deeper weekly recovery rituals.
- **Monthly rituals (time):** Account for more substantial monthly restoration practices.

C. **Projected Returns**

- **Productivity improvement (percentage):** Estimate realistic productivity gains from operating with optimal energy.
- **Decision quality enhancement (percentage):** Project how much better your decisions will be when made from a recovered state.
- **Relationship improvement (percentage):** Anticipate relationship benefits from showing up with greater presence and patience.
- **Innovation increase (percentage):** Forecast creativity and innovation improvements resulting from expanded mental space.

Case Study Two: Athlete Recovery Integration

A professional athlete I worked with was experiencing diminishing returns from training despite increasing their workout intensity. By implementing a periodized recovery strategy that matched specific restoration practices to their training cycles, we observed significant improvements in their performance metrics. Over a three-month implementation period, the athlete showed measurable gains in key performance indicators specific to their sport. Their training staff documented fewer markers of overtraining, including improved heart rate variability and reduced inflammation markers. Perhaps most importantly, they remained injury-free during this intensification phase, whereas their previous training cycles had typically resulted in minor injuries requiring training modifications. The athlete reported feeling stronger and more capable during competition, with noticeably improved recovery between training sessions.

Matching your recovery practices to your performance demands creates optimal conditions for sustainable growth. This matrix helps you design recovery approaches tailored to specific performance phases rather than applying generic restoration techniques regardless of context. For each performance period—whether high intensity, skill development, endurance building, transition, or maintenance—identify the primary stressors, resulting recovery needs, optimal restoration practices, and practical implementation strategies. Complete this matrix at the beginning of each new performance phase in your life, revisiting it whenever you transition between periods of high intensity and recovery, or when beginning new skills or projects.

Recovery Performance Integration Matrix
Match your recovery practices to your performance demands.

Performance Phase	Primary Stressors	Recovery Needs	Optimal Practices	Implementation Strategy
High Intensity				
Skill Development				
Endurance Building				
Transition				
Maintenance				

FINAL RECOVERY REFLECTION: CREATING YOUR SUSTAINABLE SYSTEM

Like maintaining healthy synovial space, recovery is an ongoing practice, not a destination. The goal isn't perfection—it's creating sustainable systems that support your long-term well-being and growth.

The recovery systems you've explored in this chapter don't just prevent burnout—they create the conditions for your most meaningful and sustainable growth. By integrating these practices into your daily rhythms, you establish the foundation for all other aspects of movement. Rather than seeing recovery as separate from achievement, you now understand how it serves as the essential counterpart that makes lasting transformation possible.

Key Chapter Takeaways

1. Recovery is not optional but essential for sustainable performance.
2. Strategic restoration requires personalized, systematic approaches.
3. Boundaries protect capacity rather than limit potential.
4. Prevention is more efficient than emergency intervention.
5. Recovery evolves alongside performance demands.

Your Immediate Next Steps

1. Complete the Comprehensive Capacity Assessment.
2. Identify your primary recovery barriers.
3. Implement the Daily Recovery Check-In.
4. Develop your Emergency Recovery Protocol.
5. Schedule your first intentional recovery practice.

Commitment moment: What recovery practice will you implement within the next twenty-four hours?

Practice:

Implementation time:

Expected benefit:

Support needed:

Remember: Your capacity for sustainable performance is directly proportional to your commitment to strategic recovery. As we move into chapter 7, we'll explore how to create meaningful collective movement, building on the foundation of personal restoration you've established.

SEVEN

FROM INSIGHT TO INTEGRATION:
A CASE STUDY IN MOVEMENT

A REAL-WORLD APPLICATION OF THE EIGHT PILLARS

Who This Chapter Is For

- Individuals ready to see the methodology in practical application
- Those who learn best through concrete examples
- Anyone wondering how this would work for their specific challenge
- People seeking to connect theoretical understanding to daily practice

Key Transformational Outcomes

By the end of this chapter, you will be able to do the following:

- Understand how to apply the eight pillars to a significant life restriction
- Learn to identify connection points between different pillars
- Develop a framework for addressing your own challenges
- Build confidence in implementing the Synovial Space methodology

THE INTEGRATION CHALLENGE: SARAH'S CAREER CROSSROADS

Let's follow Sarah, a forty-two-year-old marketing executive who feels trapped in a role that no longer aligns with her values and strengths. After fifteen years in corporate environments, she's experiencing physical symptoms of stress, emotional exhaustion, and a deep sense that she's meant for something different—yet financial obligations and fear of the unknown keep her locked in place.

This scenario resonates with many high achievers who find themselves at similar crossroads: successful by external standards but feeling internally restricted. Let's walk through how Sarah applies the Synovial Space methodology to transform this restriction into movement.

Step One: Comprehensive Assessment: Mapping the Restriction

Sarah begins by conducting a full Eight Pillars Assessment, revealing how her career restriction connects to all dimensions of her life.

Physical pillar: Chronic tension headaches, disrupted sleep patterns, and decreased energy reflect how her body is responding to misalignment.

Mental pillar: Racing thoughts about work dominate her mental space, limiting her creativity and ability to think clearly outside of professional contexts.

Emotional pillar: Frustration, anxiety, and occasional numbness have become characteristics of her baseline emotional state, with brief moments of joy appearing only during weekends.

Spiritual pillar: A persistent sense of meaninglessness surrounds her work, and she feels disconnected from her deeper values of creativity and service.

Professional pillar: Despite experiencing external success, her internal experience is one of constraint and performing rather than authentic contribution.

Relational pillar: Work demands have created distance in her key relationships, with quality time consistently being sacrificed for professional obligations.

Financial pillar: Like golden handcuffs, her substantial income supports her lifestyle but creates dependency that limits perceived options.

Purpose pillar: A growing gap between her daily activities and what feels genuinely meaningful has created a sense that she is living someone else's life.

Step Two: Identifying Connection Points: The Systematic View

Rather than seeing these as eight separate problems, Sarah recognizes the interconnected nature of her restriction.

- Her physical symptoms aren't merely health issues but manifestations of professional misalignment.
- Her financial concerns aren't just about numbers but about her need for security and how she defines value.
- Her relationship limitations connect directly to how she allocates her time and energy.
- Her mental restrictions reflect deeper questions of purpose and meaning.

Key insight: By mapping these connections, Sarah discovers that trying to address her career dissatisfaction through professional changes alone would likely fail—the restriction spans all pillars and requires an integrated approach.

Step Three: Finding the Movement Point: Where to Begin

Like finding the right joint mobilization that creates cascade effects throughout the body, Sarah seeks the strategic intervention point that would create maximum movement throughout her system.

Through her assessment, she identifies the Purpose Pillar as her primary restriction point—the place where creating space would naturally influence all other dimensions.

Guided Reflection

What truly matters to you beneath external expectations?

Where do you feel most authentically aligned when external pressures are removed?

What contribution would feel meaningful even if no one ever recognized it?

Sarah realizes her deepest values center around creative problem-solving and mentoring others—elements that are present but marginalized in her current role.

Step Four: Creating Initial Space: The First Movement

Rather than immediately quitting her job (which would create financial restriction), Sarah implements a progressive space creation strategy.

Daily practice: She establishes a twenty-minute morning ritual connecting with her authentic purpose before entering performance mode at work.

Weekly boundary: She protects one evening per week for a creative project unrelated to her career, giving herself permission to explore without productivity expectations.

Monthly experiment: She initiates one small purpose-aligned activity each month, such as volunteering as a mentor in a community program, taking a class in a field that intrigues her, or having exploratory conversations with people who are working in areas that interest her.

Key implementation principle: Begin with movements that are small enough to sustain consistently but meaningful enough to create a genuine shift.

Step Five: Expansion Across Pillars: The Integrated Approach

As space in her purpose pillar expands, Sarah implements targeted practices across all dimensions.

Physical pillar: She introduces a body scan practice to recognize tension patterns that signal misalignment, followed by specific mobility exercises for her most restricted areas.

Mental pillar: She develops a thought-capture system to identify habitual worry patterns, gradually replacing them with purposeful reflection questions.

Emotional pillar: She creates a "feeling inventory" practice to recognize and name emotions throughout the day, increasing awareness of what activities generate different emotional states.

Spiritual pillar: She integrates brief meaning-connection moments throughout her day, linking current activities to deeper values wherever possible.

Professional pillar: She initiates conversations about shifting her role toward more mentoring responsibilities, gradually reshaping her position.

Relational pillar: She establishes technology boundaries that create undistracted connection time with important people in her life.

Financial pillar: She develops a detailed understanding of her actual needs versus wants, creating a transition fund that expands her future options.

Purpose pillar: She documents evidence of impact when engaging in meaningful activities, creating a tangible record of fulfillment that strengthens her resolve.

Step Six: Navigating Resistance: The Inevitable Challenges

As with any significant change, Sarah encounters both internal and external resistance, including the following:

- Self-doubt about whether meaningful work is realistic
- Financial fear about a potential change in her income
- Identity confusion as her self-concept shifts
- Social pressure from colleagues who sense her changing priorities

Rather than fighting these resistances or retreating from them, she applies the Synovial Space principle of working with restriction rather than against it.

- She acknowledges doubts as natural protection mechanisms rather than as judgments.
- She creates detailed financial scenarios to replace vague fears with concrete planning.
- She develops a transition identity that honors both her current reality and her emerging self.
- She practices authentic communication about her evolution with selected colleagues.

Key principle: Resistance offers valuable information about your system's needs rather than evidence that you should abandon your path.

Step Seven: Sustainable Development: The Ongoing Journey

Three months into her practice, Sarah's landscape has visibly shifted.

- Her physical symptoms have diminished as her alignment of purpose has reduced her stress.
- Her mental clarity has increased through regular connection to her authentic values.
- Her emotional range has expanded beyond the anxiety-numbness pattern.
- Her professional conversations have opened possibilities for evolving her role.
- Her financial clarity has reduced the perceived risk of potential changes.
- Her relational quality has improved through more present engagement.
- Her purpose alignment has created natural energy that supports all other dimensions.

Rather than arriving at a final destination, Sarah has created a sustainable process of ongoing evolution. She continues her practices, adjusts them as her landscape changes, and recognizes that authentic movement is not a one-time transformation but a continuous journey of creating space within life's inevitable restrictions.

YOUR PERSONAL APPLICATION

Sarah's journey illustrates the Synovial Space methodology in action—not as abstract theory but as practical application to a common life restriction. While her specific circumstances may differ from yours, the principles remain consistent.

1. Comprehensive assessment reveals how restrictions connect across all dimensions.
2. Strategic intervention at key points creates movement throughout the entire system.
3. Small, consistent practices create more sustainable change than dramatic gestures.
4. Working with resistance rather than against it transforms obstacles into information.
5. Integration across all pillars creates holistic transformation rather than isolated improvement.

Practical application exercise: What significant restriction in your life most limits your movement?

- Identify one area where you feel most constricted or stuck.
- Map how this restriction affects each of the eight pillars.
- Discover the connection points between different dimensions.

- Determine which pillar, if addressed, would create the most significant system-wide movement.
- Design one small, sustainable practice to begin creating space in this area.

YOUR MOVEMENT BLUEPRINT

The following framework helps you create a personalized plan for addressing your identified restriction, applying the principles you've seen demonstrated in Sarah's case study.

Thirty-Day Movement Blueprint

Week One: Assessment and Awareness

- Complete your Eight Pillars Assessment, focusing on your primary restriction.
- Document specific ways this restriction manifests across all dimensions.
- Identify one daily awareness practice related to your primary restriction.
- Implement this practice consistently for seven days.

Week Two: Initial Space Creation

- Design one small but meaningful movement in your most restricted pillar.
- Implement this space-creating practice daily.
- Note any shifts or responses across other dimensions.
- Adjust your approach based on what you observe.

Week Three: Expansion and Integration

- Add one complementary practice in a connected pillar.
- Continue your initial space creation practice.
- Document unexpected movements or insights.
- Identify resistance patterns that emerge.

Week Four: Sustainable Development

- Review your journey and document key learnings.
- Design your next thirty-day blueprint based on your experience.
- Identify support resources needed for continued movement.
- Establish a consistent rhythm for review and adjustment.

THE JOURNEY CONTINUES

Your exploration of the Synovial Space methodology doesn't end with this book—it evolves into an ongoing practice of creating movement within the beautiful complexity of your life. The principles and frameworks you've discovered provide not just temporary solutions but a comprehensive approach to sustainable transformation.

Just as the synovial spaces in your joints create the possibility for physical movement, the spaces you create across all eight pillars enable authentic expression of your unique potential. By honoring both your restrictions and possibilities, you develop not just isolated capabilities but an integrated capacity for meaningful movement.

Remember: Your limitations aren't obstacles to overcome but invitations to discover new forms of movement that are uniquely available to you. The spaces that seem most restrictive often contain the seeds of your most profound gifts.

As you move forward, may you discover movements that surprise and delight you, challenges that strengthen you, and contributions that fulfill your deepest purpose.

Your transformation begins now.

Commitment Moment

What restriction will you begin creating space around in the next twenty-four hours?

Restriction:

First small movement:

Implementation time:

Why this matters to you:

APPENDIX: PRACTICAL TOOLS AND TEMPLATES

SYNOVIAL SPACE ASSESSMENT GRID

Set aside thirty to forty-five minutes to complete this comprehensive assessment. Consider breaking it into two sessions if needed, completing four pillars at a time.

Date:

Name:

Rate your current space in each pillar (1–10).

(1 = highly compressed/restricted, 10 = optimal space for movement)

Physical Pillar

Key restrictions:

Available movement:

Connection to other pillars:

Mental Pillar

Key restrictions:

Available movement:

Connection to other pillars:

Emotional Pillar

Key restrictions:

Available movement:

Connection to other pillars:

Spiritual Pillar

Key restrictions:

Available movement:

Connection to other pillars:

Professional Pillar

Key restrictions:

Available movement:

Connection to other pillars:

Relational Pillar

Key restrictions:

Available movement:

Connection to other pillars:

Financial Pillar

Key restrictions:

Available movement:

Connection to other pillars:

Purpose Pillar

Key restrictions:

Available movement:

Connection to other pillars:

Overall System Assessment

Most restricted pillar:

Most fluid pillar:

Where creating space would create greatest impact:

Three Priority Areas for Space Creation

1.

2.

3.

Weekly Space Creation Tracker

Week of:

Name:

Daily Movement Practice

	Monday	Tuesday	Wednesday	Thursday	Friday	Saturday	Sunday
Morning Check-In	☐	☐	☐	☐	☐	☐	☐
Movement Practice	☐	☐	☐	☐	☐	☐	☐
Recovery Windows	☐	☐	☐	☐	☐	☐	☐
Evening Integration	☐	☐	☐	☐	☐	☐	☐

PILLAR FOCUS ACTIVITIES

Track your space creation activities in each pillar this week.

Physical:

Mental:

Emotional:

Spiritual:

Professional:

Relational:

Financial:

Purpose:

RESTRICTION AND SPACE ANALYSIS

Where did you feel most restricted this week?

1.

2.

3.

Where did you create new space?

1.

2.

3.

What patterns did you notice?

1.

2.

3.

What adjustments will you make next week?

1.

2.

3.

SPACE CREATION STRATEGY

Date:

Name:

Focus Pillar

Current State

1.

2.

3.

Current Restrictions

1.

2.

3.

Root Causes

1.

2.

3.

Impact on Other Pillars

1.

2.

3.

DESIRED MOVEMENT

What movements could feel more authentic?

1.

2.

3.

How would this benefit your overall system?

1.

2.

3.

What would become possible?

1.

2.

3.

SPACE CREATION STRATEGY

Small, Immediate Steps (Next Forty-Eight Hours)

1.

2.

3.

Medium-Term Actions (Next Two Weeks)

1.

2.

3.

. . .

Longer-Term Development (Next One to Three Months)

1.

2.

3.

SUPPORT RESOURCES

What tools will help?

1.

2.

3.

Who can support you?

1.

2.

3.

How will you track your progress?

1.

2.

3.

IMPLEMENTATION TIMELINE

Start date:

First review:

Adjustment point:

Integration review:

INTEGRATION FRAMEWORKS

Synovial Space Integration Framework

Date:

Name:

Cross-Pillar Connection Mapping

Draw lines between related elements, and note how they influence each other.

Physical ⟷ Mental ⟷ Emotional ⟷ Spiritual
$\updownarrow$ $\updownarrow$ $\updownarrow$ $\updownarrow$
Professional ⟷ Relational ⟷ Financial ⟷ Purpose

Key Connections I've Noticed

1.

2.

3.

How Changes in One Area Affect Others

1.

2.

3.

DAILY PRACTICE PLAN

Morning Space Creation Ritual (Five to Fifteen Minutes)

1.

2.

3.

Day Flow Check-In Points

1.

2.

3.

Evening Integration Practice (Five to Fifteen Minutes)

1.

2.

3.

WEEKLY REVIEW STRUCTURE

Day and time for weekly review:

Key Questions to Ask

1.

2.

3.

Areas to Assess

1.

2.

3.

Adjustment Strategy

1.

2.

3.

. . .

Monthly Evolution Strategy

Focus for This Month

1.

2.

3.

Space Expansion Goals

1.

2.

3.

System Adjustments Needed

1.

2.

3.

Next Evolution Point

1.

2.

3.

Personal Movement Story:

Pillar:

My journey with _____ began when:

1.

2.

3.

.   .   .

The restrictions I've experienced include:

1.

2.

3.

The spaces I've successfully created are:

1.

2.

3.

My current movement patterns look like:

1.

2.

3.

The new movement I want to create is:

1.

2.

3.

How this connects to other pillars:

1.

2.

3.

EXPERIMENTATION FRAMEWORKS

Space Creation Experiment Log

Experiment number:

Date:

Pillar:

Experiment (Small Action to Create New Space)

1.

2.

3.

Hypotheses (Expected Effects)

1.

2.

3.

Implementation Details (When You Will Try This)

1.

2.

3.

How often?

What support do you need?

1.

2.

3.

. . .

How will you remember?

1.

2.

3.

Observations (What Actually Happened)

1.

2.

3.

Physical Sensations Noticed

1.

2.

3.

Emotional Responses

1.

2.

3.

Impact on Other Pillars

1.

2.

3.

Learning (Insight Gained)

1.

2.

3.

Next Experiment (Refined Approach)

1.

2.

3.

Follow-up date:

HABIT FORMATION TOOLS

Habit Stacking for Space Creation

Instructions: Identify existing habits you perform consistently, then attach new space-creating practices to them. Use this template to design your habit stacks.

Morning Stacks

After I _____, I will _____ for _____.

After I _____, I will _____ for _____.

After I _____, I will _____ for _____.

Midday Stacks

After I _____, I will _____ for _____.

After I _____, I will _____ for _____.

After I _____, I will _____ for _____.

. . .

Evening Stacks

After I _____, I will _____ for _____.

After I _____, I will _____ for _____.

After I _____, I will _____ for _____.

Space Creation Practices to Consider

- **Physical:** Joint mobility practice, movement flow practice, posture reset
- **Mental:** Brief meditation, thought capture, perspective shift
- **Emotional:** Feeling identification, expression moment, heart-centered breathing
- **Spiritual:** Gratitude practice, purpose reminder, value alignment check
- **Professional:** Skill development, contribution acknowledgment, boundary setting
- **Relational:** Connection moment, appreciation expression, boundary check
- **Financial:** Resource awareness, value alignment, flow check
- **Purpose:** Meaning moment, alignment check, contribution acknowledgment

Implementation Tips

- Start with just one or two habit stacks until they become automatic.
- Make the new practice so small it's almost impossible to skip.
- Celebrate successfully completed habit stacks.

RECOVERY DESIGN TOOLS

Recovery Rhythm Planner

Design your optimal recovery patterns using this framework.

Daily Recovery Practices

Time	Recovery Practice	Duration	Pillar Addressed	Implementation Strategy
Morning				
Midday				
Afternoon				
Evening				

Weekly Recovery Rituals

Day	Recovery Practice	Duration	Pillar Addressed	Implementation Strategy
Monday				
Tuesday				
Wednesday				
Thursday				
Friday				
Saturday				
Sunday				

Monthly Reset Practices

Week	Reset Practice	Duration	Pillars Addressed	Implementation Strategy
Week 1				
Week 2				
Week 3				
Week 4				

Personal Recovery Inventory
Physical Recovery Practices

Practice	Effectiveness (1–10)	When to Use	Implementation Notes

Mental Recovery Practices

Practice	Effectiveness (1–10)	When to Use	Implementation Notes

Emotional Recovery Practices

Practice	Effectiveness (1–10)	When to Use	Implementation Notes

Spiritual Recovery Practices

Practice	Effectiveness (1–10)	When to Use	Implementation Notes

COLLECTIVE MOVEMENT TOOLS

Community Space Assessment

Group:

Date:

Rate the current space quality in this community (1–10).

(1 = highly compressed / restricted, 10 = optimal space for movement)

Physical Space

Key restrictions:

Movement opportunities:

Enhancement strategy:

Mental Space

Key restrictions:

Movement opportunities:

Enhancement strategy:

Emotional Space

Key restrictions:

Movement opportunities:

Enhancement strategy:

Connection Quality

Key restrictions:

Movement opportunities:

Enhancement strategy:

• • •

Developmental Space

Key restrictions:

Movement opportunities:

Enhancement strategy:

Purpose Alignment

Key restrictions:

Movement opportunities:

Enhancement strategy:

Community innovation tool: This experiment structure helps communities test new approaches in low-risk ways before committing to full implementation. The systematic documentation process captures learning from both successes and failures, creating an evolving wisdom base that informs future direction. Use this for trying new gathering formats, decision-making processes, or connection practices.

COLLECTIVE MOVEMENT EXPERIMENT

Experiment number:

Date:

Group:

Space Creation Intervention

1.

2.

3.

Hypotheses

1.

2.

3.

Implementation Approach

1.

2.

3.

Participant Preparation

1.

2.

3.

Observations

1.

2.

3.

Group Response

1.

2.

3.

Learning

1.

2.

3.

Next Steps

1.

2.

3.

Follow-Up Dates

1.

2.

3.

ADDITIONAL RESOURCES: RECOMMENDED READING BY PILLAR

Physical Movement

- *Becoming a Supple Leopard* **by Dr. Kelly Starrett:** Comprehensive guide to optimizing movement, addressing pain, and preventing injury with accessible techniques for all fitness levels.

- *Pain-Free: A Revolutionary Method for Stopping Chronic Pain* **by Pete Egoscue:** Simple yet effective approach to understanding the body's interconnectedness and creating sustainable pain-free movement.

- *The Body Keeps the Score* **by Bessel van der Kolk:** Explores how trauma affects physical movement patterns and offers science-based approaches to reclaiming bodily awareness.

- *Deskbound: Standing Up to a Sitting World* **by Dr. Kelly Starrett:** Essential reading for professionals dealing with the physical limitations of modern work environments.

Mental Space

- *Thinking, Fast and Slow* **by Daniel Kahneman:** Explores two systems that drive our thinking and how awareness of these patterns can create mental space for better decisions.

- *Mindset: The New Psychology of Success* **by Carol Dweck:** Fundamental understanding of how our beliefs about abilities affect our capacities for growth and learning.

- *Deep Work* by **Cal Newport:** Strategies for creating focused mental space in a distracted world—essential for professionals seeking depth.

- *The Obstacle Is the Way* by **Ryan Holiday:** Stoic philosophy applied to modern challenges.

Emotional Intelligence

- *Permission to Feel* by **Marc Brackett:** Science-based approach to developing emotional awareness and regulation from Yale's Center for Emotional Intelligence.

- *Atlas of the Heart* by **Brené Brown:** Maps the connections between emotions and experiences, creating language for navigating emotional territory.

- *Emotional Agility* by **Susan David:** A practical framework for navigating emotions as data rather than as directives.

- *The Language of Emotions* by **Karla McLaren:** Reframes challenging emotions as messengers carrying actionable information rather than as problems to solve.

Spiritual Development

- *Man's Search for Meaning* by **Viktor Frankl:** Classic exploration of finding purpose through restriction.

- *The Power of Now* by **Eckhart Tolle:** Accessible approach to presence that transcends specific religious frameworks.

- *The Art of Possibility* by **Rosamund Stone Zander and Benjamin Zander:** Transformative practices for creating new paradigms of possibility in everyday life.

- *Anam Cara: A Book of Celtic Wisdom* by **John O'Donohue:** Poetic exploration of spiritual connection that respects personal journeys while offering universal wisdom.

Professional Growth

- *Range: Why Generalists Triumph in a Specialized World* by **David Epstein:** Celebrates the power of diverse experiences.

- *Designing Your Life* by **Bill Burnett and Dave Evans:** Design-thinking approach to career development that embraces constraints as creative catalysts.

- *The Practice* by **Seth Godin:** Framework for meaningful professional development through consistent, authentic action rather than through seeking perfection.

- *Principles* by **Ray Dalio:** Systems approach to professional excellence through continual improvement and honest assessment.

Relational Space

- *Nonviolent Communication* by **Marshall Rosenberg:** Essential framework for authentic expression and deep listening that creates relational movement.

- *The Five Love Languages* by **Gary Chapman:** Accessible introduction to different modes of connection that helps readers navigate relationship patterns.

- *Attached* by **Amir Levine and Rachel Heller:** Science-based approach to understanding attachment patterns that influence all relationships.

- *Difficult Conversations* by **Douglas Stone, Bruce Patton, and Sheila Heen:** Practical guide for navigating challenging interactions while maintaining authenticity.

Financial Movement

- *I Will Teach You to Be Rich* by **Ramit Sethi:** Practical, psychology-based approach to creating financial systems that align with your personal values.

- *The Psychology of Money* by **Morgan Housel:** Explores the emotional and psychological aspects of financial decisions, aligning with your holistic approach.

- *Your Money or Your Life* by **Vicki Robin and Joe Dominguez:** Transformative perspective on the relationship between resources, time, and purpose.

- *The Simple Path to Wealth* by **J. L. Collins:** Straightforward approach to financial independence that reduces complexity and creates sustainable systems.

Purpose Development

- *Designing Your New Work Life* by **Bill Burnett and Dave Evans:** Practical framework for creating purposeful work within existing constraints.

- *Let Your Life Speak* **by Parker Palmer:** Gentle exploration of finding purpose through listening to your authentic self rather than external expectations.

- *The Crossroads of Should and Must* **by Elle Luna:** Visual and written inspiration for making choices aligned with authentic purpose.

- *Ikigai: The Japanese Secret to a Long and Happy Life* **by Héctor García and Francesc Miralles:** Accessible introduction to finding purpose at the intersection of passion, mission, profession, and vocation.

ONLINE RESOURCES AND COMMUNITIES

Movement Practice Groups

- **Functional range conditioning (FRC) community:** Online collective of practitioners sharing approaches to mobility development based on scientific principles.

- **GMB fitness community:** Supportive group focused on natural movement patterns for sustainable physical development.

- **The Ready State:** Kelly Starrett's resource hub for movement optimization with extensive video library and supportive community.

Skill Development Platforms

- **Coursera's "Learning How to Learn":** Science-based approach to developing learning skills that are applicable across all pillars.

- **MasterClass:** High-quality instruction from world experts across multiple domains, perfect for multidimensional development. (Stephen Curry's masterclass is worth the subscription all by itself.)

- **Mindvalley:** Personal growth platform with structured programs across physical, mental, emotional, and spiritual dimensions.

Community Support Networks

- **Modern Elder Academy community:** Support network for life transitions and purpose development at midlife and beyond.

- **The Junto Institute:** Leadership development community integrating emotional intelligence with business acumen.

- **Wisdom 2.0:** Community exploring mindfulness integration into modern life and work environments.

PROFESSIONAL SUPPORT DIRECTORY

Movement Specialists

- **Functional range systems (FRS) practitioners:** For addressing mobility restrictions through scientifically-based joint health approaches.

- **Postural Restoration Institute (PRI) practitioners:** For addressing the body's inherent asymmetries to optimize functional movement and reduce pain.

- **Certified strength and conditioning specialists (CSCS):** For translating improved mobility into functional strength and performance.

Mental Health Professionals

- **Cognitive behavioral therapists:** For addressing thought patterns that create mental restriction.

- **Acceptance and commitment therapy (ACT) practitioners:** For developing psychological flexibility within existing challenges.

- **Mindfulness-based cognitive therapy (MBCT) specialists:** For integrating awareness practices with cognitive approaches.

Financial Advisers

- **Fee-only financial planners:** For unbiased guidance on creating financial systems aligned with your personal values.

- **Financial therapists:** For addressing emotional patterns that impact financial decision-making.

- **Certified financial transitionist (CeFT):** For navigating major life transitions with financial implications.

Spiritual Guides

- **Secular spiritual directors:** For nondenominational guidance in exploring meaning and purpose.

- **Mindfulness teachers:** For developing present awareness practices that enhance spiritual connection.

- **Philosophical counselors:** For examining life questions through structured exploration rather than through religious frameworks.

ABOUT THE AUTHOR

Raphael St. James is the creator of the Synovial Space methodology—an existential framework for finding sustainable movement potential despite life's real and perceived restrictions. After being diagnosed with osteoarthritis at a young age, he obtained his New York massage therapy license and personal training certifications in 2005 to understand and manage his condition.

Over three decades, Raphael built an expansive operations management career across luxury hotels, spa management, and flexible workspaces while simultaneously pursuing acting, improv, and activism. When regulatory barriers blocked his vision to transform his avocado orchard into a permaculture food forest and limited his mobility seminar offerings, these restrictions became the catalyst for him to develop a system for navigating around life's brick walls rather than ramming into them. This system ultimately became the Synovial Space methodology.

As a New York licensed massage therapist (NY #018143) and certified personal trainer with extensive business experience, Raphael synthesizes anatomical knowledge with practical wisdom about navigating the interconnected systems of body, business, and client care.